The Coming
of the Ages

The Coming
of the Ages

Craig B. Wood

Writers Club Press
New York   Lincoln   Shanghai

The Coming of the Ages

Writers Club Press
an imprint of iUniverse, Inc.

For information address:
iUniverse
2021 Pine Lake Road, Suite 100
Lincoln, NE 68512
www.iuniverse.com

ISBN: 0-595-19088-X

Printed in the United States of America

Acknowledgements

I want to thank my wife, Karen, who endured much during the writing of this book. She has never fully understood my work. Yet our marriage has been a wealthy experience, providing me with the stable home base previously lacking in my life and I love her for many and diverse reasons.

Charlie Ketcham, a firm and solid friend, has been a rock of Gibraltar in a sometimes high rolling sea.

James Bestick and Don Humbarger served as examples to me of common sense morality and human integrity as well; some of who and what I am must have come from them.

Eldon Lake, like Gandalf, has been a quiet guide and an ever-present mentor.

Gracious support came from Tim Hurd and his wife, Nancy Montgomery, and I love the both of them simply for being who they are.

Diane Ramsperger and Wallace Long were helpful editors, and most of their perceptive commentary found its way onto these pages.

The reference staff at the Springfield, Oregon Public Library was competent, diligent and very generous with their time.

Ruth, Bruce and Christopher, my sister and brothers, were always patient with me during times when their patience must have been sorely tried.

A large personal regret is that my father and mother, Parkhurst B. Wood and Martha Jane McCormack, did not live long enough to know that there was more in me than mischief and errant nonsense.

Far above and beyond all others has been the assistance of my friend, Linda, as an amanuensis. She was loyal, persevering and absolutely necessary. This book could neither have been begun nor finished without her. Planets and even whole star systems could be named after Linda and that would not be honor enough. May all her wishes come true and let heavenly grace attend her forever.

Contents

Preface

Whence do you come, *Homo sapiens*, and wither do you now go hence? In the great chain of Being, who are you and what is the purpose of your animal growth? Face to face with the inexperience of your Human youth, poised and caught between the two extreme possibilities of extinction and a universe of fresh discovery, where do you go from here, and why?

Human history is a many varied tale, a tapestry interwoven with countless threads of people and events. Since the time of our genesis, billions of the Human child have moved and breathed upon the Earth. The progress of Human history has been but the natural growth and fulfillment of Human evolution, and of the emerging awareness of Human thought and mind. Great empires, kingdoms and dynasties, diverse and fabled realms as they have been, have always risen and held power for a while and then crumbled into dust, yet always to be replaced and freshened by the progress of species maturation. Large wars have been fought, with significant battles won or lost. Political, economic and religious theories have had their various times in the sun.

Heretofore these many lives and deeds and thoughts and words have all shared one common thread which has run true since the very first day. And that thread is this: That whatever has occurred so far has occurred upon this one island planet, this Earth of our beginning. Up until this time everything that has happened or has been done, so far as Human history is concerned, has happened or been done right here at home, on Earth.

In this regard, there has been but one event of Human history that is truly unique, and that was when the first step was taken by a Human being upon the surface of the moon. For the first time ever in Human history, Human feet have walked upon a celestial body other than Earth.

Thus this deed must be more than just another routine event of life going on as before. Instead this is, and must be, an omen. This is and must be a sign that great change is here, a signal to *Homo sapiens* that a movement of species-wide significance is upon us and has now begun. No other explanation for the turmoil and total confusions of these days is possible, but that a new and as yet unknown season of the Human mind is coming into climate.

In the book of **Revelation**, taken from the New Testament of the Christian bible, it has been written,

> "To him that overcometh will I give to eat of the hidden manna
> And will give him a white stone,
> and in the stone a new name written,
> Which no man knoweth saving he that receiveth it."
> **(Revelation of John** 2:17.)

That white stone is the moon. There is simply no other white stone of any such significance on the scene today, not now or ever before. The moon is now given to Humankind, and is hereby named as Luna. This was our first step into the void that surrounds Earth. This first step signals, and must summon forth in full biological force, the start of Human puberty and the beginning of our adolescent stage of growth, and of our movement into a darkness whose dark we shall one day outgrow and leave behind. Thus this day comes in fulfillment of ancient prophecy and must therefore be answered in full, answered by this generation of the Human child.

And what is the evolutionary movement that is now occurring? Observe the pattern of growth this species has already followed. First, however, let us note the life cycle of a single Human being.

In the beginning the man and the woman lie down with each other, and so mingle together in sweet love. The father impregnates the mother with his seed, and she conceives the new child within the womb of her belly. There follows a time of gestation within the mother's womb. Then comes the birth of the baby, the infancy, the childhood, puberty and adolescence, adult maturity, old age, then death and rebirth. Now when you look at our species as a whole organism you can appreciate that the growth pattern of the species entire must resemble, in a larger way and in the galactic sense of species maturation, the smaller growth pattern of the individual. I say again, and this must be the thesis statement for **The Coming of the Ages**: That the biological life cycle of the individual Human being is repeated, paralleled and mirrored, in the galactic sense of species development, by the larger and greater development of *Homo sapiens* as the species entire.

To answer the will of Creation our sun first came into fire, and the several planets were made from gasses and bits of matter spewed forth and spun outwards from the newborn star. The space around the fresh star was filled to bursting with electrical fire, magnetic and gravitational forces in fullest expression, and with waves of solar radiations expanding all over the place. The newly formed Earth was covered with waters that were warmer then but which have since cooled. Thus when the heat of the fires and the light of the sun lay upon the waters of Earth's ocean, the father lying upon the mother in order to fulfill the will and the purpose of the Creation, Mother Earth was impregnated with Creation and life was then conceived in her ocean womb. Millennia passed during that age of Human gestation, and in those days our bodies first took solid form, and living thought first came into the Human mind.

Gradually the waters cooled and shark predators were many. Eventually, discomfited by the colder waters and pursued by stronger, faster predators, our amphibious ancestors migrated from the ocean so as to live on dry land. The time of that migration was the birthing of *Homo sapiens*, the movement from the environs of warm water onto solid ground.

The growth continued. Our younger, infant ancestors could not walk erect and had no spoken or written language, and took such shelter as they could find in caves or upon the open plains. This aeon was the time of Human infancy.

Gradually, and as the child grows away from its infancy *Homo sapiens* learned to walk erect, developed spoken and written language skills and gained a basic knowledge of tool usage. Thus it has been with the Human species: That the building of the first ancient civilizations on this planet represents the first solid works of the Human childhood, while our landing on the moon represents the highest flower and fruit of that selfsame blooming, continued and always ongoing.

During this age we have moved from family clans to tribal villages to city-states and onto the present day rule of the world by nation-states. We have filled the Earth to its limits. We have walked upon the moon. *Homo sapiens,* as a species, has been a growing child up until now. What else could this walking upon Luna mean, but that the childhood is ending and that the age of Human adolescence has now come? From the building of the first pyramids to the landing on Luna has been the fulfillment of the Human childhood. Thus, *Homo sapiens* is now in the process of leaving childhood behind and entering into its teenage years.

When we view Human history with this awareness in mind we can understand, for instance, that the pyramids of Egypt and in Mexico as well as the Great Wall of China are nothing more than mud pies and sand-castles built by children at play. We can also see the glory that was Rome and the splendor that was Greece, magnificent civilizations as they seemed to be at the time, were but children's social clubs both in thought and deed. And likewise we can further know that our many and mightiest of wars have been, in truth, mere childish squabbles and temper tantrums, fought by angry children hurling curses and throwing rocks at each other.

The Women's Liberation movement has come into fruition at this time because the Human female tends to enter adolescence at an earlier age than does the male. As a species our galactic age is that of 12-year old boys and girls, now entering puberty. The landing on the moon represents the sprouting of the first pubic hair of species adolescence. The current political atmosphere of one war crisis after another, after another, after another demonstrates the normal growth pains felt by any child who is becoming adolescent.

Here, Human history and biology are well met. The time has come to GROW UP, to mature in all ways, to grow upwards and outwards from this planet, to spread the Human light upon the void. The time has come to move fast and hard forward, to solve and answer the many questions that have bedeviled these days and all former days as well. The time has come to unite ourselves as a species, and to enter this fresh and clean arena that now lies before us as a banquet newly spread upon the table has been laid before a hungry peoples.

If our Earth is overpopulated by Humankind then this solar system of planets and moons, as well as the further galaxy beyond this place, is not. The first thought of Creation has always been that you shall now go forth and multiply, being fruitful. You shall now go forth to count and name the stars until your children have outnumbered them. You shall dwell upon a million worlds or more, crossing fantastic distances at incredible speeds. You shall travel thru out the void, giving light unto the dark until the darkness is no more. In the fullness of your mature and adult growth you shall come to be, *Homo sapiens,* a species of farmers and gardeners, builders of civilization, teachers, thinkers, seekers of truth and bringers of light, and makers of fire.

Thus, with the landing upon Luna a new dawn has come and a fresh day awakens. *Homo sapiens* now rises to seek the fulfillment of its Human potential for growth. Our present need is great, heavy are our fears, and so we must rise. Yet the fire of the Human soul burns with a strong flame, pure and clean, and so we rise. We are the hopes and the dreams of Humankind, and so we rise. *Homo sapiens* was born to grow, and Human evolution is far from its conclusion, and so we rise. There is much to be done, much that only we can do, and so we rise. Thus let the awakening soul within the Human breast now begin to reach upwards and outwards from this planet which has been the cradle of Human birth.

Remember, that "to be or not to be" has always been the only question, and shall always be the only answer as well. And wherever you may find yourself, however great be the web which entangles you, however cold and black the night may be, also remember that your salvation lies within you. The shining dawn is here, the sun shines upon a new day, and so now you go forth.

Chapter 1:

Technology

Homo sapiens, the Species Entire

As we enter this stage of growth, as *Homo sapiens* has now taken the first steps into the solar system and thence into the outward galaxy, it is necessary that we know exactly who and what we are, where we are, and the purpose we are struggling to achieve. We are a species of animal, named *Homo sapiens* and known among ourselves as Human beings, mammals of the Humanoid family. As individuals, most of us are less than two meters taller than a bug on the ground. Our home planet of Earth is only slightly larger than a Ping-pong ball. Our sun is a medium-sized star on the outer rim of a galaxy which might contain a billion or so of similar stars. And this galaxy is but one of many.

The pyramids of Egypt and the Great Wall of China, greatest works of the Human childhood, are less than five thousand years old. Not so very long ago in our history of knowledge the profoundest Human thinkers believed the Earth to be a flat surface rather than ovoid in shape, or that the sun is in orbit around the Earth and that Earth itself does not rotate upon its axis. If our landing upon Luna signals the beginning of Human adolescence, then all of our beliefs, our knowledge, our scientific theories and religious fervors are based upon the life experience of 12-year old children. And that is what we are, *Homo sapiens*, born in sexes of male and female: A 12-year old child who has just left home for the very first time and is now afraid of what dangers might be waiting out there in the unknown dark; and yet we are also very eager to continue the game, to climb the next highest rung of the ladder, and to take more steps forward.

The larger purpose of Human history is that we must now grow into our adolescent phase, that we shall grow and achieve adult maturity in due course, and that the Human soul shall one day fulfill its potential for

Godhead, the Christ fulfilled and unveiled, and be one with the Maker of all life. Yet for today we have but one duty and highest hope, and that is to grow up, to grow up, AND TO GROW UP. Today we are young boys and girls, inexperienced and innocent of deliberate sin, born to seek the adult maturity which still lies before us.

But consider: That if we once crawled up and out from the womb of Earth's ocean so that we now walk erect and upright upon the dry land of this planet, and if all the glories of our recorded history are but the logical extension of that first crawling step, then how much greater glory and beauty and truth shall come to pass because of this new first step now newly walked upon Luna? *If we have come so far as this since our earliest struggles up unto dry land, then how much further shall we travel hence-forth, and where else might we go, and what might we find and how much more shall we learn as a result of this new step upwards?*

Humankind can make this forward motion! For we are one body made from many bodies, one mind filled with the thoughts of many minds. We have many hands with which to work, and many feet to walk and run, for we are the flesh and blood of the gathered Family of *Homo sapiens*, the species entire. We are less than one millionth of an inch away and scarcely a nanosecond back from taking those next steps which must enthuse and inspire this coming of the ages, that we might grow and mature fully into this first millennium of our adolescent development as a species of truly sapient beings.

A Complex of Problems,
and Questions of Actions

Homo sapiens is the most successful user of tools ever to live on this planet. We are able to acquire various skills in the making and the using of tools so as to move matter and manipulate energy, and thus do we build and maintain and expand Human civilization. We have now come to a time, however, when our technologies are powerful enough to remove us from the game board as a species, to extinguish our fire, to give us a young and premature death of species extinction. If the industrial polluting of Earth has been caused by an inexperienced misuse of Human technology, then the only remedy for this global problem is, and must be, that we as Humankind shall clean this planet of those poisons and build for ourselves a stronger and a cleaner set of tools, so as to learn from our mistakes by correcting them. It is both the duty and the desire of this generation of *Homo sapiens* that we shall be the cleansers of the Earth, and that we must build the foundation for any Human civilization yet to come.

There are some among us who have so far understood neither the global nature of this problem, the very hugeness of the threat, nor the glorious success that a global struggle for survival must surely engender. "Sweet are the uses of Human adversity," as Shakespeare once wrote, and never shall such words be proved more true than upon this occasion and with this particular adversity in mind. For in building a cleaner, stronger technology and in learning how to clean this planet we shall gain new strength from our current weakness, new knowledge from our current ignorance.

Already there are clear indications that all is not right. The birds of the air, for instance, can no longer give birth to their chicks in good health because their reproductive abilities have been damaged by pesticides in the food that they eat, so that their offspring are poisoned even before they hatch. Likewise, huge amounts of fish caught by commercial fisheries show visible signs of cancers and of other diseases. Many parts of the ocean which were once thick with fish have now become barren and sparse of yield, while many millions of dead fish are being washed ashore on various beaches and coastlines every year. And these millions of dead fish, and the dead baby birds also, have died from diseases which we do not yet understand.

Similar epidemic diseases are beginning to run wild among our domesticated livestock, and this has been the case with the Mad Cow disease in England as well as with the diseased chickens in Hong Kong, and these must surely be the precursors of the worse and even worser troubles that are yet to come. Because of various poisons released into the atmosphere and dropped into the ground and into our rivers, we are losing our topsoil as well as our groundwater. When these are gone there will be the end of all agriculture, the finish of all farming and organized food production. In many of our larger cities the air we breathe has become so fouled, so dirty and nasty, that a person can actually see the dirt being breathed in and out. Even the ozone layer of Earth's atmosphere, miles above the planetary surface, has been damaged by our carelessness to the point where the temperature of this planet has begun to rise against us.

All of these conditions have begun to affect us individually. Unexpected deaths due to cancer, heart failure and brain-stroke are increasing everyday. Our children are being born deformed or diseased or both. Supposedly healthy people are dying left and right from unknown causes. The rates of suicide, drug addiction and chronic drunkenness are at a terrible level of yearly and even daily increase. Human life on this planet is becoming an ugly thing, vomitocious in the extreme, producing widespread insanities within the general populace. Do we all now understand the global threat involved, that life has become cheap on our own homeworld and is a squalid affair more often than not, nowadays?

Even the basic biology of *Homo sapiens* has already been damaged. The reproductive abilities of man and woman are being sickened and made weak by the environmental toxins in the air we breathe, and in our food and water supplies as well. If neither impregnation nor conception can occur with any strength of purpose or desire, if too many pregnancies begin to miscarry or produce idiot offspring, and if we cannot reproduce ourselves in good health and with a certain knowledge of a fresh and springtime growth yet to be, then all is lost.

All is lost and lost forever unless we can cleanse our environment, this planet, of the poisoned brew we have made for ourselves by our young and inexperienced use of tools. Do we not see, do we not yet understand, can we not appreciate that if we take no cognizance of this situation then Human history ends now or very soon, and that everything that has happened or has been done up until now will have been done in vain? Let us try and live now, *Homo sapiens*, and try to live with the idea of our own good health in mind, so that there can be some hope of physical salvation and the reclamation of the Human soul.

A hint, to the wise, should be sufficient for action. What we have been so calmly giving to ourselves up until now, and so calmly accepting as well, have been less like mere hints and more like a series of hammer blows delivered to the Human head in full force, sledgehammer blows coming from the hands of an immature and untutored child named *Homo sapiens*. Even the rainwater is no longer clean, but has been tainted with chemical acids. Whole forests of trees in Europe, Canada, the US of A, in every nation of Central and South America and in all the woodlands of Asia also, are beginning to waste away from the effects of this acid rain which we have let fall upon them. Are we so eager to have our home planet denuded into a premature baldness of trees and forest? How many hints and signs and other ill omens do we need to see, anyway, before we finally begin to take action?

These have not been quiet problems. On the contrary, like a forest of squealing pigs they have made their presence well known among us, a mad stampede of noise and foul odors that seems to be worse and then grows worser as time goes by. Just how many alarm bells do we need to hear ringing, anyway, before we start to take note of the fear, and of the cause for the fear? Having received so many compelling warnings, *Homo sapiens*, and being aware of our surroundings, when do we plan to make our move? When does the action start? When do we plan to make our move, *Homo sapiens*?

Homo sapiens is now well placed in harm's way by basic problems of our own making, and the evidence of this is here before us, clear and simple. So I must ask again, and not just to satisfy an idle curiosity but in response to an urgent and terrible demand: When does the action start? I MUST ASK AGAIN AND WE MUST ALL ANSWER: WHEN DOES THE ACTION START? WHEN DO WE PLAN TO AWAKEN FROM THIS SLEEPING STUPOR? WHEN WILL WE BEGIN TO MAKE POLLUTION GO AWAY?

Do we finally begin to see that Human existence, the very lifeblood of Humankind itself, is now face to face with the worst and most serious problem ever met in our young career? Without healthy food, water and air this species cannot survive. We cannot and shall not survive on this planet, I tell you, without good food, water and air supplies to sustain us. Do we seriously believe that we can violate all the basic laws of existence and commit any offenses which might seem to amuse us, and then hope to survive the attempt? Do we really believe, in our own deepest heart of hearts and in the essence of the Human soul that such is the case, that *Homo sapiens* can defy and so blatantly challenge with impunity the Maker of the stars?

Or, concerning this question of industrial polluting, would it be more truthful to say that we have so far been lazy, morally weak, slow to take action and less than fully wise? Would that be a more truthful statement to make? Do we not believe that it might be better for ourselves, *Homo sapiens*, to wake up now, to wake up now and to fight for our place among the stars with all the strength and courage and wit we possess? We have been summoned towards the Light of the stars in the night, and that is the call which we must answer today.

In the book of **Revelation**, taken from the New Testament of the Christian Bible, it has been written,

> "To him that overcometh will I give to eat of the hidden manna,
> And will give him a white stone, and in the stone a new name written,
> Which no man knoweth saving he that receiveth it."
> (***Revelation of John*** 2:17)

That white stone is the moon. There is simply no other white stone of any such significance on the scene today, not now or ever before. The moon is now given to Humankind, and is hereby named as Luna. This was our first step into the void that surrounds Earth. This first step signals, and must summon forth in full biological force, the start of Human puberty and the beginning of our adolescent stage of growth, and of our movement into a darkness whose dark we shall one day outgrow and leave behind. Thus this day comes in fulfillment of ancient prophecy and must therefore be answered in full, answered by this generation of the Human child.

We must all surely see that this is no joking matter, no election year issue raised merely for the sake of political orations, no minor problem that will just pass away if ignored. There is a basic proposition now before us: That we will either wake up and do our duty or we will die now and die young, young and unknown and unfinished. We are the children of Creation: Our inspired life has been nurtured by the Earth as our mother and we must either rise to seek the fulfillment of our Human destiny or we must and shall perish as a species.

Yet even as we now stand, naked and surrounded by darkness, not knowing what to do or where to go from here or why, we shall see a path of light before us, a bridge of shining light. It has been written that, "Where there is no vision the people perish." Herein let our vision of

Human growth be refreshed, so that even in the midst of dark blindness we shall see again, to know the light eternal.

Oil

Constant change is among the most fundamental conditions of all life. If the Earth has become polluted then it must be ourselves, boys and girls, who are at fault here. Therefore it follows that it must be ourselves, *Homo sapiens*, who must clean away any mess that has been made. This means that a total change of Human thought and behavior is now in order. This is, in fact, a question to be answered during these early days of our adolescent maturing, on a species-wide level of housecleaning knowledge, and with the purpose of learning how to manage with success a planetary ecology.

For instance, we must now say farewell to the widespread use of petroleum as a source of fuel. First, the amount of oil available is shrinking every day, and will not increase. Since the Earth itself is not a large planet, as planets go, just how much more oil can there be?

Second, the fumes and gasses produced by the use of oil as a fuel are poisonous, fatal to the health of our kind. Already the air we breathe has become discolored and dirty, giving a stinking smell to the cities and countryside alike. Hospital beds are filled with dying patients, while the cemeteries become more clogged with dead bodies everyday. And, think ye, who will be the next to die? Just take note that everywhere and in every place, and all around you wherever you might happen to be at the time, and especially in the large cities, how so many people cannot speak an entire sentence without coughing and hacking. So hateful has Earth's air supply become that in its toxic stench, the air seems more and more to be like a poisonous gas rather than the very breath of life itself. All of this comes from the excessive dependency upon oil as a fuel, and that dependency must be ended and left behind.

Third, the very scarcity of oil brings the threat of internal warfare within the species. The need for more oil was one of the prime causes for the Great War which swept thru Asia and Europe during the 20th century, burning like all Hell broken loose and doing heavy damage to cities, nations and even to whole continents. Since then smaller wars have been provoked and a larger war must surely come to pass, if these same conditions continue to prevail. Are we certain that we wish to find ourselves in a position wherein nations are throwing nuclear bombs at each other, wherein men, women and children must die in millions, wherein Human civilization is bombed and burned back into some perverted type of Stone Age, and all for the sake of oil?

To do these things for the sake of a fuel source which will soon be used up and gone anyway, which produces poisons that are deadly to all life on this planet, and this fuel is too awkward and cumbersome to be carried across the seas with any assured safety for the nearest beaches and local fishery waters — does that seem wise to anybody here? I mean to say that while moneyed wealth is one thing to be considered, and that the influence of political power must also be considered, but that global stability and the avoidance of species suicide is the great question that has been laid upon this generation of *Homo sapiens*, both as our Human duty and as the desire to perform a great work for ourselves. Let us not just calmly read on but stop here, and answer the question, ANSWER THE QUESTION! *Please, please, please you good sirs and ladies, we must answer this question!*

Does this seem wise to you, *Homo sapiens*? Does this seem wise, that Human history should be so thoroughly threatened by the industrial need for a fuel that has always been dirty from the very first get-go? Who wants that stuff, anyway? Who needs it? Are there not other fuels available, fuels that are cheaper, cleaner and more abundant? Geo-political realities demand that the use of oil as an industrial fuel be ended and eschewed forthwith. *The individual Human being is the most inventive creature on the face of the Earth, so let us get busy with invention, get busy now.*

The chief cause of the polluting on this planet has been the automobile. The automobile industry must retool itself, must wean itself from petroleum fuels in the same way that a child is weaned from its mother's milk. Even more so because in this case the particular milk involved, oil, is toxic to all Humankind and to our homeworld also. Do we not yet understand? This planet, Earth, is the only place now known and available to us that is suitable for Human habitation. Thus this planet must be made safe from all threat, and any other considerations are of a secondary priority at this time.

The automobile can be built to move with the power of electric or solar or other batteries. In fact, the people of Brazil use ethyl alcohol which is distilled from sugar cane as a fuel, and this is both non-polluting and also less expensive to produce, refine and transport than petroleum fuels ever could be. Or we can make a Sky-car that is made to fly thru the air along fixed highways of magnetic levitation, and these Sky-cars can run with the power of hydrogen fuel cells, and so we can remove the cumbersome congestion and traffic of these heavy automobiles from the bare surface of Earth, and from our cities and countrysides also.

Such questions are no longer open to further discussion: This industrial polluting of Earth must cease; therefore the common use of oil as a fuel of industrial work and output must also cease; and therefore the internal combustion engine must be remade so as to work with a cleaner fuel and thus help to cleanse and make healthy the ghastly and squalid pigsty this planet is fast becoming.

Transport and Carriage

There are far too many automobiles in use right now, for that matter. The main streets of every large city on Earth, and also the many wide freeways leading towards and away from them, are already clogged into total constipation by these billions of cars in motion everyday. This system of individual transportation by automobile has multiplied upon itself so much that personal transport and carriage are being hindered, or even blocked all together.

Nowadays, it is a fact that even a badly lamed dog can crawl or limp the length of a city block more quickly than any resident of New York city can travel the same distance by car. This being true, and the truth of the matter should be quite clear to one and all by now, then we have no system of personal transport and we are losing our cities as well. Surely, we can do better than this.

In America, for instance, just take a look at the traffic constipation in Seattle, Washington. During the daylight hours no one can move in that city except in slow and halting motion, so thick is the congestion of the streets. During the rush hours, when people are traveling to and from their various jobs, bumper-to-bumper car traffic extends for more than 20 miles from the city limits. And this condition is occurring on the widest of freeways and interstate highways. Because of its geographical location, no thought of any broader growth for Seattle is realistic. Thus Seattle has been caught in a stranglehold, and the strangulation is being done by the sheer weight and bulk and number of cars on the road.

In case there might be some thought among us that the traffic conditions in Seattle are in any way unusual, then let us think again. Think again, and be smarter this time! Let us think again, as we look at San

Francisco and at Los Angeles and at Dallas and at Houston. Think again as we look at St. Louis and at Chicago, where the same conditions of constipated transport blockage prevail with massive and stupid force to seriously hinder the comfort and convenience of our own city systems. Think again as we look at Kansas City, and then look at Atlanta, GA also. Think again as we look at Miami, at Philadelphia, at Boston, and at Washington, DC. To look at a real mess of constipated, gasoline crap then simply visit the oil-smogged city of Detroit, US of A, where so many of those cars were and still are being built in the first place.

These are our cities. These cities, and in the countryside as well, are where we live and breathe. Can we not then do better than this? Can we not build better places than these are, *Homo sapiens*, and make a better home for ourselves? Of course we can, and we must and we shall, for this is a natural part of our growth as the species entire. We are a maturing species, and this type of industrial growth is but a part of the maturation process from childhood into the Human adolescence. But as native instincts for survival begin to express themselves and to take precedence within our thoughts, conversations and in our daily actions, we shall move ourselves to do the work.

If we wish to look further abroad then let us look at Montreal, Mexico City, London, Paris, Rome, Vienna, Berlin, Tokyo, and at Moscow, and at Beijing, and at Jerusalem, Mecca, and New Delhi, where all the same conditions now flourish in a false exuberance of unreal and crazed industrial prosperity. Just look at Tehran and at Baghdad! Just look ye at Calcutta, where Mother Teresa lived and died, if you wish to see a true pesthole of Human filth. Just look you at Venice, where the canals have become no more than diseased cesspools of stagnant Human waste.

In Bangkok we see a city that was once filled and alive with sweet Oriental beauty, but has now become a place where the canal rivers flow with waters that are so dead that not even the fish can swim in there in good health. In Hong Kong we find a vast and open sewage system of pestilence and stench where once there was a thriving city of bursting light and Human life, so great and terrible is the damage being done both to our centers of Human population and even unto the very center of the Human soul itself by gasoline fumes and other industrial pollutants.

If purposeful movement is a sign that conscious life exists, then those cities are dead or dying things. Surely, and with an utmost sense of Human purpose, we can do better than this. When the foxes make clean lairs for themselves, and so do the bears, and when birds make clean nests for themselves, and when honeybees maintain their clean hives then it must follow, and naturally so, that we Human beings can build and maintain the clean health of the cities wherein we dwell.

Just look at the grimy dirt being produced by those cars! Look at the filthiness in the air that we breathe. Look at the greasy soot that smears and defiles our buildings and our lives and even our very souls. Even the snow that falls upon a winter wonderland, and this snow that was once clean and sweet, and pristine with a crystalline delight of clear freshness, has become nasty and dirty because of all this oily stuff in the air. Our rivers and lakes have become so polluted with petroleum chemicals that some of them have actually caught fire.

Moreover, these oil fumes are corroding and ruining all our city structures and architecture, both modern and ancient. Sidewalks and stores, houses and tall buildings as well as churches, schools and banks alike, and all other things made of concrete or brick or granite materials are being crumbled and eaten away by the acid effects of petroleum gasses in the air that we breathe.

There is a strong need here, therefore, to rebuild and refurbish all the large cities on Earth during the next one hundred years. This time around we must build our Human cities with the health of Human beings in mind, rather than for the convenience of cars and automobile traffic. We shall build our cities, with our jobs closer to our homes, and thus we shall move beyond the problems of massive individual transportation altogether and beyond the use of oil as an industrial fuel for Humankind.

Already the coliseum of Rome, the Sphinx in Egypt, as well as structures of elder beauty in Athens, Kyoto, Lisbon, Beijing and Mexico are being damaged almost beyond repair by chemical and industrial pollutants. If such works of stone, ancient as they are, can be so harmed in this way then just imagine how much worse damage is also being done to the delicate tissues of our Human lungs and hearts and brains in the same deadly way. If the Great Wall of China, Stonehenge and the Lincoln Memorial cannot endure the oily grease in the air we breathe, then how can any of us? The use of oil has produced the worst blight ever seen on this planet, and there can be no progress nor any move forward whatsoever in Human history until we have learned how to shun that stuff completely.

There is no greater need on this planet, on this Earth which is now filled to bursting with so many great needs, than the need for a means and method of transportation and Human carriage which does not require the use of an internal combustion engine fueled by petroleum gasoline. Just as even a large sponge can absorb only so much water before it becomes water soaked and saturated, and then the sponge can absorb not a drop more of water, then in the same way this Earth can absorb only so much manufactured poisons before the planet dies and loses forever the capacity to nurture and generate any further life. We know, and we have known for quite sometime now, that such is the case: That there is a need for a global healing to be done here, that our homeworld must be refreshed and made clean, and that the Human usage of tools must itself be completely retooled, to be forged anew and made better by our own conscious effort of deliberate will.

Why, therefore, have we not yet acted? Thousands upon thousands of newspaper and magazine articles have been written, countless political speeches have been made, and in our personal conversations we have heard that various changes are needed and that the time for great change is already here.

Yet so far, no such great change cometh. No change is being done; no healing of Earth has yet started to occur, at least not by any deliberate effort of *Homo sapiens*. So far there has been a lot of anxious talk, a lot of verbal stuff and nonsense, and a bunch of foolish excuses made with no actions in mind or with any real work yet begun, and these exertions have been nugatory and morally lazy almost to the point of Human dead-head-edness. Up until now there have been only small signs and indications that any of us are even aware that there is, in fact, any direct threat to the survival of our species. Such knowledge, when finally understood by one and all, should and must command the full attention and eager duty of the whole body of the Human family.

What has gone wrong with us, *Homo sapiens*, and why have we been so slow to act in this crisis? Why have we so far refused to act against this obvious threat? Why have we, up until now, been unable or unwilling to move forward? Can we not go on from here? What is the purpose of being alive, of living as Human beings, of being members of an animal species which is endowed with the potential for creative intelligence, if we cannot act to save ourselves when the time for saving action is so clear and so present, so huge and blatant before us? What is the use of discussions if no one listens and learns from the discourse? What is the use of writing books, if no one reads them? Are we mere clods of dirt waiting to be stepped upon? Or are we living creatures who, possessed and enthused with the vital fire of animal struggle and animal strength and animal intellect, now seek to reach towards the stars above with the full hope in the search for higher light?

We must continue as we have begun, boys and girls. We must always struggle for our survival and towards our fuller fruition. And if some corporate businesses or national industries must be remade and reformed so as to fit into the future growth of *Homo sapiens*, then let it be so and let it be done. These various people who run those corporations are, after all, likewise desirous of life and of healthy living. Some business enterprises must pass away, necessarily and inevitably so. But we can find other work to do and other business enterprises to take their places. Above all, we must move. We must move now, we must awaken and be alive to the power and the glory of a greater growth for the Human child.

Homo sapiens has been observing and enduring this problem of industrial pollution long enough. The time for thought and action towards a purposeful growth of the Human soul is here and now upon us, and demands a response from every Human being now alive within the species entire. So stand up! You shall stand up and stand higher! We must stand up and get off our fat derrieres and move, move and move faster, to move with purpose and will and direction towards a distant goal which we do not yet fully understand but which always shines before us nevertheless, as the very idea of eternal light.

The individual Human being is the most inventive creature on the face of the Earth. And so let us make ourselves be busy with invention, right now, and with no more wasted time or excess talk involved. The basic question is this: Do we see and understand the present danger? If so, then do we wish to launch some type of an effective response to this threat, or must we be caught and destroyed as an example of a failed species, as *Homo sapiens* extinct? The Dodo birds were slow and stupid in their day, and just look at where they are now. Do we wish to join them in their extinction, or do we wish to one day write our name upon the cores of stars and distant suns?

With such thoughts as these in mind, for instance, let us no longer fool ourselves with any stories and public discussions we hear concerning the use of any smog-reduction devices being installed upon the internal combustion engine. Halfway measures will not work here. In fact, because of the false hopes and complacency they generate, half measures are much worse than none. The time for any such minor, cosmetic cures has long since been passed.

Consider a large and heavy boulder, and the force necessary to roll it across a flat plain. To first move the boulder all your strength is needed, whereas once the movement has begun then much less effort is required to continue the forward rolling. The same is true with the heavy weight of industrial pollution. That boulder is here and is already in motion upon the long and sometimes rocky road of Human enterprise. Thus if the pollution caused by petroleum fuels is reduced by even as much as a full 60%, the remaining 40% will be more than enough to continue the forward motion of the polluting effects already begun. Therefore the internal combustion engine must either be remade so as to burn with a clean fire or else be abandoned altogether, so that some more efficient means of moving matter from one place to another might be found. Until we are able to invent some method of transport and carriage which does not require the use of petroleum as the basic fuel of our technology, then Human technology can have no further growth nor any faster forward motion at all, nor can Human civilization itself move with any faster speed or in any good directions.

Just as old clothes that no longer fit must be either remade or discarded, the progress of Human history as well as the physical health and spiritual well-being of Humankind require that we make a clean break away from this dependency upon fossil fuels. The very clear fact of the matter is that this Earth of ours is not big enough to hold both our cars and ourselves also. When you notice that the horse which has long been pulling your wagon has dropped down dead at your feet, and is stinking with the stench of putrescent animal flesh then that smell alone should be enough to alert you that the time has come to find a new horse. For that matter, so long as the need is here and the mood upon you, why not hitch your wagon to a rising star if you can?

And let us not waste our time in wondering whether or not such a major shifting of focus within the military-industrial complex is possible. Never has any generation of *Homo sapiens* been called upon to do that which is utterly impossible or beyond all reason. The military-industrial complex has been built by us, is maintained and worked by us, and may therefore be shifted by us according to our desires and present need. If Hannibal could bring elephants over the Alps so as to wage war against the empire of Rome, then we can do this. Just think of the job as one of sweeping dirt off the kitchen floor, and go on from there.

Power and Expansion

If we children of *Homo sapiens* are caught in a hurly-burly situation of homeworld industrial polluting wherein a new broom is most desperately needed to sweep clean the floor of the Human house, then what could be the name of that new broom?

Nuclear power, and well tamed, is one good source of that fresh fire and solar heat energy is another. We must pass the barrier of considering nuclear energy as just a way to make a bigger bomb. We cannot wage a nuclear war on our own home planet, the only planet now available for Human habitation, because where would Humankind live then, or in what type of damaged, wounded condition?

Thus our finest scientists and engineers have been wasting their time and talents, and we are squandering rare and valuable natural resources in useless effort, by building these weapons which are intended for use against our own kind in some stupid war of species suicide. The various political leaders of Humankind, captains of industry and military generals also, have not yet understood that the first footsteps taken upon Luna made a change in the Human condition entirely and forever, and the general population of the Human body politic has yet to understand this fact as well.

Nuclear energy can be made safe to handle. The stars are nothing but large nuclear furnaces, after all, and that process has been ongoing since the universe began. The full thrust of Human invention must be towards the harnessing of the nuclear flame. Much of the moneys and other wealth now being spent in nuclear weapons research and development must be rechanneled, just as excess water must be diverted from a flooding river so that the nearby villages might not be drowned and swept away.

A massive increase in our efforts to produce a controlled nuclear fusion reaction must be done and well made. This is an emergency need that must be filled. The nuclear waste so far accumulated may not be safely stored on Earth nor can that stuff be safely gathered and transported to be burned away in the sun. Think rather that this nuclear waste must be somehow processed and thoroughly recycled into quiescence. There must be, somehow and in some way, a good usage to be made with that stuff. One thing we do know right now is that untreated nuclear waste may not be allowed to further accumulate on our homeworld. Something, something definite and beneficial and productive must be done so as to make clean that poisoned mess.

This is a basic problem caused by the expansion of our investigations into the nature of nuclear physics. Either solve this basic and most necessary problem, ye sons and daughters of Creation, or else we must abandon the use of nuclear power altogether. What is this nonsense, anyway? Did we think that we could discover and employ the nuclear reaction and reap the benefit of the vast energies thereby unleashed, and then take no notice of the waste products thereby produced?

We have been foolish if we thought that such was the case. Get busy and do the job! Get busy and learn this new craft! Let us learn our craft, ye children of desire. Let us hurry to learn our craft, the craft of making nuclear fire, or else run away from that fire before we are burned too badly. Do the job or get out of the shop, and if there is too much heat in the kitchen then build a better stove.

Nuclear fire must be controlled, just as any other type of fire must be controlled. Are we silly children who are playing with fire in a dry forest or are we a serious species, a species now engaged in serious growth toward adult maturity? Can we grow and mature? Can we find new power and yet not be destroyed by the passions of that power, by the passions of that power unwisely used? Can we grow up and mature from this age, or must this species die and extinguish itself because we cannot subdue and tame a wild beast of our own discovery?

In the years ahead the nuclear wastes which have been buried under-ground or dropped into the ocean in supposedly watertight containers which, of course, are not truly watertight nor are they eternally secure from all possible leakage must be, somehow, retrieved and rendered harmless. And we shall do this for the sake of God who is the father of all true Creation, and to protect the virtue of our own mother, and she is our birth planet of Earth.

Whatever safety precautions we have taken so far have been, necessarily, primitive and uncertain. Tho we might not yet understand what errors have been made up until now, we may be certain that in such a young area of Human effort as this is, that some mistakes must have been made. To think of ourselves as the masters of this nuclear fire, the flame of which we have barely touched upon and which we have so far used only to make bigger bang-bang bombs and so as to burn away larger and larger seg-ments of our own peoples, is mere childish ignorance and foolish bravado. Nuclear power must be controlled and made useful. To do that we must first control and direct our endeavors to understand the basic nuclear reac-tion, and to think more in terms of living rather than of dying, of living rather than of bringing more fire and ruin to our own kind and to the homeworld. Instead, let us think of lighting a torch in the darkness, so as to find our way safely thru this void of supernal night.

Thoughts and desires much larger than those we have yet known must begin to occupy *Homo sapiens* now. For instance, we now have access to Luna as our stepping stone into the rest of this solar system of planets and moons. In less than 50 years from today Humankind can build and main-tain a thriving colony on Luna which is capable of producing a self-sus-taining and independent dominion of the Human house. Underground cities could be built more easily on the moon while using robotic equip-ment, since the gravity there is so much lighter than on Earth. With hydroponic agriculture we can grow vast farming gardens of trees and other foliage which are more than sufficient for our oxygen needs, as well as to provide fruit and vegetable produce for our dinner tables. Wherever we go, we can find or make our own water. Once we begin to do these things on an everyday basis, once the newness of it all becomes a matter of everyday life, then the difficulties involved will become daily routines and a joy to behold in the expansion of Human territory. With nuclear reactor plants, hydroponic farms and plasma drive engines thrusting forward, we can go anywhere we wish to go and find more room for living thru out this local sun system.

And we might very well ask, just what will those people do on Luna, living on that stark and barren island in the sky? That question states its own answer: They will live as we have always lived before, only more so. Let us stop thinking in terms of the little that has been done so far, and see instead a vision of Human expansion into virgin territory, and of life's possibilities increased far beyond all current measure.

On Luna, we shall see Human civilization being doubled and redoubled as never before. We shall see not only scientific laboratories, but farming communities as well. We shall see great universities and libraries built, as well as schools for common education. Let there be restaurants and grocery stores, banks and sports arenas built and made active, houses and vacation hotels, factories and transportation systems used, theaters and museums, gardens and lush green spaces, and Human history going on as it always has gone on before only with greater expansion, and with everything now new and fresh and clean and wide open to us and our children, and for our children's children also.

Yet such an expansion of civilization will require a massive expenditure of energy, as well as raw materials and other natural resources. Whence might these needed supplies be found? The planet Mercury, closest planet to the sun, is both the potential treasure chest of this solar system and the opening key to its lock. Observe the basic pattern of the planets in their order of distance from the sun, for this pattern is very clearly defined. The first four planets are made of solid matter, whereas the outer planets are made of frozen gasses. Now, these planets were made from gasses and bits of matter spewed forth and spun outwards from the sun during the time of its first ignition. Thus the heavier planets are closest to the sun for the same reason that a gust of wind can blow a feather farther than it can push a rock.

So it follows that Mercury, even tho a small planet, must also be the heaviest planet per cubic centimeter in this solar system. A very large portion of all the heavy metals and raw materials to be found in this solar system are in that small but very dense planet, which for *Homo sapiens* is now just around the corner and right down the street from Earth. Many of the basic materials necessary for the next few thousand years of Human civilization are now within our eager grasp.

Further, the planet Mercury rotates upon its axis in such a way that it presents the same face towards the sun for long periods of time, so that the sunny side is always very hot while the dark side is always close to the coldness of absolute zero. By planting colony cities underground so as to insulate ourselves from these extreme conditions of heat and cold, we can begin mining operations into the richest mother lode of mineral wealth ever discovered. Thus on Mercury, therefore, Humankind can build and maintain another independent colony, and we can do so with a vast increase in both knowledge and wealth.

Because the hot side of Mercury is always hot, we can lay out a massive system of heat-gathering equipment and harness the primal fires of the sun so as to fuel any industrial efforts we will ever need to make. In less than one solar day we could surely find and transmit enough electrical energy to light every city and every home on this Earth, as well as to fuel every factory for a year. Thus with the conquest of Mercury we now have a grand bonanza source of raw materials and mineral wealth parked in a side-by-side propinquity to an inexhaustible source of heat energy. Consolidated Edison, Inc. supplies the power needs of New York City every day, and with no special effort involved; therefore the planet Mercury, so near to the naked fire of the sun, should be able to provide the same type of basic energy for the whole planet Earth, naturally and forever.

The knowledge of how to gather such prizes is already known or will soon be learned; the needed technology is already here or soon will be available; and, the need for forward motion in this area is great, very great indeed. All that has been lacking up until now is the moral Will to grow upward and outward from this planet, to rise up and spring free from this cradle of Human genesis.

There might be water on Mars. Those channels on the surface of Mars, which were once thought to be canals, are evidence that there were once flowing rivers on that red desert planet. That frozen water has now sunk into the soil and can be reclaimed. If not, then we can produce our own water on the spot.

When we plant a few billions of tree saplings and other shrubbery in the Martian soil we can begin a process of greening that planet, to produce a healthy atmosphere on Mars in much less than 200 years from now. Mars could be made more like the Earth by stimulating and enhancing the atmosphere and soil conditions. This would take time to accomplish completely, but here we are dealing with a potentially living world, unlike the moon. Once we have begun such a task of planetary upbuilding, when those barren deserts have been changed into gardens and farmlands at our behest, then who knows where *Homo sapiens* might go from there?

With Human technology retooled and made better, and with the health of Earth fully restored and made clean again, then with a solid and firmly established colony on Luna, and with basic heat energy and raw mineral supplies coming from Mercury, and with room to expand and grow soon to be found on Mars, then a world of new worlds now lies wide open before us and accessible to our further explorations.

Einstein's barrier, that there can be no traveling faster than the speed of light, will certainly be evaded just as all such barriers have always been evaded or overcome in the past. When that breakthrough occurs then the whole of this vast galaxy will be available to Human discovery and visitation. Think of a fine old mansion, ancient and ageless beyond compare, whose front door has recently been unlocked and thrown open to our gaze, so that we may enter and see the wonders of this house which had been closed to us prior to now. Who knows what wonders we might find, what hidden rooms we might explore? In a universe of a billion billion stars, there is more than enough room for us to grow upwards and outwards from this small Earth of our beginnings.

Do we see now that Human history, the direction and the various goals of Human growth, has now changed? Do we understand that the Human territory has now been increased far beyond any previous measurement or limitation? Do we now understand that *Homo sapiens* has moved into an aeon of growth wherein our adult maturity might one day be achieved in great glory if only we can survive the crisis brought about by this sudden awakening, by this unexpected encounter with the onset of Human puberty, and this entry into our first millennium of species adolescence?

For now, consider these things to be true, first and foremost: That for the first time within the conscious memory of Humankind a movement of species-wide significance is being done; that global questions which demand global answers are afoot and running fast; and that only with a joyous lust for life and the happy help eagerly given by every child of this generation can we hope to go forward from today.

There is much which is beyond our current knowledge. About the origin of the cosmos, or of the reason why life exists, or as to the true meaning and cause of the seemingly random events of Human history, we are certain of next to nothing. Yet let us consider whether there are any least little things that we do know, of which we do have some knowledge, and which answers might serve us now.

We know that there are some means and methods wherein hard work might bring a fruitful reward, if only the effort were made. For has this Earth not been the very birthplace and the cradle of the Human race? And as for the stars that burn in the night, do they not burn with a fire that is kin to but less than that flame that always burns within the Human soul? For if we have built pyramids and Great Walls during the times of Human childhood, then why should we not build and ignite our own stars, and make new planets also, in the ages yet to come?

Ocean Farms, *Et cetera*

My goodness, but we are very much behind our schedule! A mere 66 years elapsed from the time of the first airplane flight in 1903 until the year 1969, when the first Human steps were taken upon the surface of Luna. During the 30 years since that event, however, very little ongoing progress has been made. Because of the various military, economic, and political tensions between the nations and the churches and the varied ethnic populations which comprise the larger family of *Homo sapiens*, we have been too concerned with face to face confrontations to have time for any practical thoughts concerning the outward expansion of Humankind from our homeworld. Also, this universe that we have now entered seems so vast and dark and unknowable to us that the very idea of any further ventures into the void has daunted us, and has subconsciously stunted both our physical and spiritual growth.

By now we should have had a dozen shuttle craft flying back and forth between Earth and the moon everyday, carrying construction crews and construction materiel, and we should be building or have built already at least one large colony city on Luna. Those efforts would give us the necessary knowledge and skills so that we could then go on to establish mining operations and solar heat collection facilities on the planet Mercury. Also we should have begun, by this time, the greening of Mars and the manufacture of a breathable atmosphere on that planet, to make for an environment that is friendly to our kind. Rather than looking back in anger and in mutual mistrust within the Human body politic, we should now be seeking to expand and to make more solid our basic position here, and to search for the primal source of those stars that are the distant lights that burn in this great ocean of night.

The problems caused by our polluting of Earth with our own inexperienced and careless use of the technologies which are the natural outgrowths of the Industrial Revolution should have been confronted by now. For instance, we need to find more food and to establish better food distribution systems so that the masses of Humanity might be well fed, lest an outbreak of food riots in the near future serves as the excuse for more war between the have and the have-not peoples of Earth. Also our cities must be rebuilt and refurbished so that they might become healthy places for living. Also our transport and carriage systems must be remade. Also the rivers, lakes, and the forest woodlands must be maintained with some sense of purity in mind, for the sake of our own needs of agriculture if for no other reason.

But all these efforts cost money, and require the expenditure of great wealth, and so we ask ourselves the question: Where shall this great wealth be found? And the answer, of course, is very simple: The war budget of every nation on Earth must be cut by 80% at least.

Verily, verily I say unto thee: *Homo sapiens*! What a wastage of time, mental strain and natural resources has the burden of war become unto us in these days! The very finest of our scientists and engineers are spending the intellect of their brains in vain; whereas the political atmosphere of one war crisis after another and then after another again, continued onward *ad infinitum* and *ad nauseam*, has caused acute paranoia to creep into our everyday thinking and conversing. We are robbing ourselves of valuable natural resources also, by this fanatic manufacture of huge weapons and weapon delivery systems with which we intend to launch the next great Civil War to be fought within the gathered family of Humankind.

What a fat load of hot crap and further nuclear crapola are we preparing to deliver upon our own heads and from our own polluted minds and thoughts, by this obsessive making of more and more war weapons that can only be used by Humankind against ourselves, and towards the conquest of what? Bethink yourselves, my children, bethink ye! What are you doing? What are you doing, and why? With the long history of Human frailty in mind, are we completely and totally convinced that the very highest use of Human tools and Human knowledge is only to build bigger and better weapons of war? Are there no further goals of Human endeavor other than this manic preparation for the suicide of our kind; and as we are a growing species of sapient beings who are endowed with the potential for creative intellect, is it good that we should try to die so young and untaught as we are now, and all for the conquest of what?

An internecine war between the nations of the East and the West, a massive nuclear bomb war which must be endured on this planet of Earth that is only slightly larger in size than a Ping-pong ball, and ourselves scarcely bigger than molecules are, is clearly foursquare against both the best interests of our own survival and the further development of our Human education into true sapience. Ergo, why should we follow such a path?

Why should we walk this path which we have walked many times before, and which leads so certainly towards thicker quicksand and hotter fires? Why should we walk that selfsame path again when, to pursue those first steps we have already walked upon Luna, we can find and follow pathways that are fresher, cleaner, and more enticing than the waging of yet another war within our species would be?

Surely the expansion of Human territory from this cradle of Earth onto the various planets and moons of this solar system, and thence further outwards towards the nearest stars, must command our interest more fully and with greater benefits than would a global slaughter of the Human family ever hope to be.

The military-industrial complex represents a concentration of corporate powers for the sake of accomplishing goals that are too large to be accomplished by individual or local efforts. This idea of concentrated and co-operating forces, and the military-industrial complex is definitely an idea rather than a solid thing or collection of things, gives to us a mighty tool which can be used in many ways. For instance, there is a need for more food growth and for better food distribution within the species. Entire continents of people are in danger of starving, and this must not be. Vast farms can be built on the ocean floor and enough food crops thereby harvested so as to feed the populations of a dozen planets.

And yet let us know now that the whole purpose of industrial pollution has been to stimulate *Homo sapiens* into the building of a cleaner and healthier Technology, so that we can learn the rules of planetary ecology, rules that must serve us well in the days to come. For this Earth is but our first planet, and the first of many more planets yet to be found. But we will not be able to live on those planets, however, unless and until we have first learned how to live here. So let us learn to be better farmers, farmers who help rather than hinder their own farm acreage, farmers who think in terms of centuries rather than in single seasons, farmers who can farm on a planetary scale of Human enterprise.

Tho Earth's ocean is vast and deep, these waters are not invulnerable. The ocean is capable of being harmed and, in fact, has been greatly wounded already. This young and careless behavior on our part has been to the serious detriment of the life and biological health of our own species, and against the health of all other living things on Earth as well. We simply cannot continue to dump billions upon a billion tons of industrial wastes and other Human filth into the ocean every year and then expect no damage to occur. Those wounds will heal themselves, no doubt, if we do no further harm and act instead as bringers of refreshment, as agents of cleansing. So therefore let us stop using the ocean as a toilet bowl, and stop pouring poison into the very waters of the planetary womb wherein we were engendered as *Homo sapiens*.

Guard the planet of the Human birth. Let this be the duty of what is now known as the military-industrial complex of the species: ***to protect and encourage the healthy growth of Humankind.*** There is no need, for instance, for Human starvation to occur upon a planet so filled with food. There is more that can be done with the military-industrial complex than the waging of war within the species. There are different battles to be fought, and other wars to be won. One of those battles, to end the threat of worldwide starvation by farming the ocean, is now here before us.

How is it that we have such a shortage of food supplies here, while at the same time we have built and continued to build this massive overabundancy of weapons on our own homeworld?

Against whom do we intend the use of these weapons? Is it possible that we have built these big weapons only so that we might use them against the peoples of our own kind, and upon this small world of our common native birth? How foolish this is, and how childish such behaviors have been up until now!

To make war within our own kind, to lay waste our own homeworld for reasons which we regard as most significant and divine but which are, in fact, of juvenile and hooligan significance only, and to bomb into submission these nations whose civilization might make all of Human illumination shine the brighter, and to burn cities and whole nations to the ground, and to fill the air with the stench of Human corpses for the sake of truth and liberty and justice for all, and while at the same time we disregard and try to ignore the basic damage that has been done to the Human soul itself, as well as to brush aside the miseries and the grief caused by such wars, is very stupid stuff indeed.

Observe those animals known as porcupines, and how those sharp quills which constitute their main defense against aggressors are always pointed outwards, sharp and fine and pointed away from their own bodies. How is it that we of *Homo sapiens*, and we are presumably as smart as or smarter than those porcupines are, have built our own weapons to be pointed backwards against ourselves? Do we not see, and do we not recognize the significance of the fact, that all of our weapons are pointed backwards against *Homo sapiens* as the physical body politic and *spiritus mundi* of the species entire? Do we wish to destroy our own planet? Do we wish to destroy, with nuclear fire and poisoned gas attacks, the continents of North and South America, as well as Europe and Asia, and Africa and Australia also, as well as to do harm to the penguins and the polar bears of

Antarctica also, as well as to the dolphins in the sea and the eagles in the air, because of the mere fact that we are so youthful, ignorant, and afraid of each other that we cannot somehow learn to manage our Human affairs more wisely and with greater success?

Everyone should know by now, or at least we should have vaguely sensed, that with our landing and walking upon a planetary body other than Earth for the first time in Human history we have passed a significant turning point in the biological growth of our kind. And as children soon begin to think beyond their former childish passions when they come to feel the onset of their own maturation into adolescence, then just so must *Homo sapiens* as the species entire do likewise. All of our industrial efforts which have been built for the manufacture of war and war materiel must now be converted towards cleansing away the industrial polluting of our homeworld and the simultaneous expansion of Humankind outwards from this cradle of Earth. Those same factories where tanks, artillery pieces and nuclear missiles have been made before can now be shifted and changed in design so as to make the basic tools and other stuffs which are needed for the outward spread of our kind.

Let us imagine a mighty cannon, the largest cannon ever built. This cannon can deliver accurate fire against distant foes when the need is there, and we have used this cannon many times during all the various wars of Human history, and this cannon is very like unto the corporate entity which we now refer to collectively as the military-industrial complex.

But now the enemy has changed position, and is no longer stationed on this hill over here but has now moved onto that hill over there, so that the aim of this cannon must be turned according to the new target that is now in sight. Indeed, the same old enemies might have themselves been replaced with new enemies and new targets, and the same old war might not be the same, not at all the same, as this new war might yet prove to be. Therefore, in order to accommodate these changes of history, this same old cannon of united Human effort must itself be repositioned and reaimed, in allowance for the changing needs of an ever-growing Human awareness of our Human condition. Ergo the new thrust of our big cannon must not be aimed towards the conquest of our fellow Human beings, but must instead be shifted and aimed towards the exploration and colonization of the outer spaces from Earth for the sake of all Human power and expansion, so that the species entire might grow and expand and fulfill itself into higher maturity.

In the film **_2001: A Space Odyssey_** we see Human activities taking place upon a giant space station which has been made in the shape of a great floating wheel. This flying space port is but a roadside inn that is parked in orbit somewhere between Earth and Luna, a place where all space vessels are coming from or going to their various destinations, a lounge of rest and relaxation, a laboratory for scientific observation also, and a post of military preparedness as well, of course. We must now build such a way station for ourselves so as to have a launching pad out from Earth and towards the various planets and moons of our local system. Talk about making something that is larger than the greatest pyramid ever built! This would be the largest moving thing ever made by Human hands, and could be one of the wonders of ancient Earth when viewed by our posterity of 3,000 years from these times.

As we are building our space wheel, and as we are cleansing both the dry land and the ocean of Earth from industrial pollutants, as we are reforging all of Human technologies so that they might burn with cleaner flames, and as we are expanding up and outward from this Earth, we shall establish the foundation for an interstellar civilization that might endure beyond the crumbling into dust of any monuments of ancient stone that we have carved in past days.

Yes, and we could make such movements, and we could change our own lives for the better, but all our funds, natural resources and everyday conversations are now frozen behind a glacier wall of slow-moving, cold war politics and policies. All our moneyed wealth is frozen just as our basic political positions have been. All of our wealth is being spent in the manufacture of war machines, but now we must move our attention into other areas. These people who have grown wealthy from the building of war weapons will not starve because of this shift in Human attention; rather, we can all gain even greater wealth during this expansion of *Homo sapiens* territory. There is great wealth to be made, and long term wealth at that, during the upbuilding and further growth of Human civilization.

These war industries are stagnant, and cannot produce any further fruit except by the waging of more civil war of internecine rage within the Human body politic. That goal is, by itself, a dead-end street of no return. The first step which we walked upon Luna has changed everything. Nothing is the same anymore. We are not, in fact, the same peoples who we were a century ago. We have landed and walked upon the moon, and so we must now stand taller and see further than we have stood or seen up until now, and also we must learn to think with wider, deeper thought.

We are users of tools; and until our minds have sufficiently grown with the coming of Human maturity, the tools we now possess must satisfy our current need. But for now, we have the tools and we have the will to use them rightly, and we have the desire to thrive and flourish from here. The only problem, then, is that we must use the right tools so as to fulfill the proper Human will, and this we shall do, and thus we shall answer the primal urge of our basic Creation, and most truly so. Surely, if we can feed the peoples and clean the Earth, and if we can seek the fire and the light which is beyond the stars around us, that is effort enough.

Forestation, and Hemp Growth

For instance, from the knowledge gained in public discussions and debate and thru common gossip also, we are all very much aware that Earth's forests and other foliage groups are under attack due to the expansion of industrial outgrowths. Gutted and ravaged by long habits of wanton over-logging, these forests are crucial to the health and natural balance of the planet and so must now be restored to fullest and most vigorous growth, guarded and protected at all costs. These forests of trees are much too valuable to be chopped down for the sake of mere lumber.

The people most concerned with the moneyed interests of the logging and lumber mill industries must be able to see further and more clearly than they have seen up until now. There are better ways to make money than by harming the very planet where that money is to be spent and enjoyed and further invested. How can *Homo sapiens* go on from here, on to Luna and thence to the planets and the stars beyond, seeking wealth such as the Human race has never dreamed of nor even imagined before, unless we first secure and make solid our homeworld position?

The homeworld must be made safe and healthy before Humankind can even hope to grow upward and outward from this place. Thus this question involves not only the moral virtues of cleanliness and true thrift but also the economic fact that a healthy landscape provides more room for natural financial profits to be made.

In Homer's <u>The Odyssey</u>, following the sudden, brutal and very well-deserved deaths of those rash and arrogant young princes who had plundered and dishonored the great house of Odysseus during the years of his long absence, the hero spoke thus unto prudent Medon, saying "Courage: my son has dug you out and saved you. Take it to heart, and pass the word along: Fair dealing brings more profit in the end." Three thousand years later the same question is again uppermost: With whom should we deal most fairly and for what greater profit, if not with ourselves and for the prosperous health of this, our Earth, and to make a secure and stable base whence the rebirth of any further enterprise and species advancement might yet come to be done?

The root structure of the trees holds together the topsoil of the planet, without which there can be no organized agriculture, no system of food harvest, and is therefore a *sine quo non* for the health of both the planet and for ourselves. The photosynthesis which occurs in the forests replenishes the oxygen content of Earth's atmosphere. Breaking down wood fiber into wood pulp at the paper mills causes the vomiting of chemicals into the rivers which kills the fish, poisons the river waters and damages the topsoil near the river banks. Furthermore, the sudden removal of an entire chunk of forest must send out shockwaves upon the land which, even if we do not yet fully understand their final effects, cannot be good. To be blunt, without full and healthy forestation all the law and order of nature is being ruined, and to the point of utter desolation and grief for every living thing on Earth.

Also it simply takes too much time, too many years, to restore and renew an axe-savaged forest. Hauling those massive logs to the mill and processing them into lumber and other wood products is an awkward business, cumbersome at best. Considering the long hours of hard labor involved as well as the damage done to the breathable atmosphere, and also to the topsoil and the water supply, any financial profits gained by the world's lumber industry are quite meager when compared to the larger losses obtained. Yet the fact remains that many good people depend on the lumber industry as their source of livelihood, and so what are they now to do?

To answer this vital economic problem and to fill this very real Human need, a global restoration of hemp-plant cultivation is now in order. We already know that a time for major change in Human output is here, so let this be one of those changes. Let this, the certainty that the hemp plant is easily able to fill any void brought about by a reduced and much more firmly controlled lumber industry, be one of those least little things that we do know, of which we do have some knowledge.

Hemp, which was once a cash crop of enormous value, has been scarcely grown in recent years because of various political reasons which were all just a batch of stuff and nonsense that should now be cast aside. The public reason for the ban on hemp agriculture has been that one or two strains of the hemp plant produce marijuana, which has been used for centuries as a pleasure drug by unwary lotus-eaters. Alas, because the true reason for the ban on hemp farming, of course, is that various chemical companies and forest owners wished to close down and stifle all competition to their own financial interests, financial interests which were then and are now based upon their ownership of forest lands, lumber mills and wood pulp processing plants.

In effect as well as in reality, then, those makers of great wealth have suffered huge economic losses during the ensuing decades as a result of that ban. For lo and behold, while the cash value of a woodland forest might be great indeed, the potential cash value of hemp farming is much greater even so. Thus these bankers and business owners, who might have been smarter and more farseeing, have been content to gather only nickels and dimes where they could have had rubies and fat bags of gold coins instead.

The fact of the matter is that those people who wish to grow marijuana plants can easily do so in secret, and no public law will stop them if they are sufficiently determined. More to the point, however, is that the global economy is now very much in need of active stimulation, so that a change of attitude towards hemp agriculture must now be considered.

Like a newly discovered wonder drug which can cure any number of hitherto untreatable diseases, a return to the cultivation of the hemp plant can answer a multitude of questions and solve many problems.

Hemp is easily grown, strong and sturdy in the soil, and one of the most prolific plants found on Earth. For instance, if you leave a single

Douglas fir tree to stand alone in the middle of a field for a year, then at the end of that year you will still have the same tree standing alone plus a few saplings perhaps. A male and a female hemp plant growing side-by-side in the same field, on the other hand, will produce a whole field of hemp during that same year.

The hemp root structure is such that it strongly holds the topsoil in place and acts to prevent soil erosion. Furthermore there is a chemical interaction between hemp growth and minerals in the soil, and this interaction serves to maintain the nitrogen content of Earth's oxygen-nitrogen atmosphere.

Hemp seeds contain an oil that can be used both as a lubricant and as a fuel. Also they possess a protein content as high as that of the soybean.

There are medicinal qualities of hemp, having to do with the relief of physical pain, anxiety stress, blood circulation problems and stomach disorders which need to be further explored.

Hemp fiber is the strongest natural fiber known, much stronger than either flax or cotton, and makes a very good thread, rope and cloth. This knowledge, by itself, should be worth the ticket price of admission so far as the world's textile industries are concerned.

The paper made from hemp fiber is of a far higher quality than that made from wood pulp, and was used as the paper whereon the rough drafts for both the American Declaration of Independence and the U.S. Constitution were writ. In short, Human industry can produce more useful goods from one acre of hemp plants than from four acres of trees, including the making of board lumber.

If all these statements be true, and they are true, then is there anyone out there in the book-reading public or from the farming and business communities as well, who can see any economic benefits that might be gathered and further increased by an active pursuit of hemp agriculture?

Because, the national economies of the world are now in a desperate position of apparent stalemate, the numbers of unemployed people as well as the rates of inflated money value have been and still are on a constant level of increase. Much of our industrial output has become repetitious and boring, as stagnant as a dead-end street can be.

How many nations are there who are top-heavy with their national debts because of these conditions? Wedded and habit-formed into the manufacture of bigger weapons and more elaborate weapon delivery systems, while eschewing the growth and manufacture of healthier and more useful produce, the global economies of the nations and thence of the species entire are moribund. Moving fast in no other direction but than in a downward spiral, we are headed straight towards a ground zero level of both moral and financial bankruptcy. The rebirth of hemp agriculture represents an attempt to enter into new areas of economic endeavor which must, in and of itself, encourage further business and other industries all across the fiscal board.

These constant legal battles over forest conservation are time-wasters, money-costers and excuses for anger. They need to be ceased for those reasons alone, and will be ceased on the instant that an eager commitment to hemp-plant agriculture is made by the lumberjack industries of the world, and with a wisdom gained from the pressures of economic necessity. Above all, insofar as Earth's ecology is concerned, we need action, action, and more actions now and forthwith. In the history of the world there has never been any fort so strongly attacked as is now the case with our fortress Earth, and we ourselves are the attackers.

There is no other answer but that the major industrial polluters of this planet must themselves repent of their errors and make remedial movement towards the health of Humankind. Also to be considered, and this is a question that has been asked at least once before within the long reach of Human memory, "What should it profit a man if he shall gain the whole world but lose his own soul?" Where is the profit with money, and wealth and political power if the species should die or be enslaved or be so weakened and confused as we are now? Where then would be the fun and enjoyment of life, and the normal growth as well?

Enough of this lollygagging about! Cease and desist with the legal folderol, the endless debates and pointless quibbles, the varied procrastinations which just go on and on and on, and get thyselves busy with good work instead! Stop sucking on one thumb while sitting on the other, *Homo sapiens*, and do something! Let us do the job that only we can do. And what is Humankind, anyway? Are we a race of quick and living beings or are we mere blobs of inert matter and dirt clods? Can we recognize a dangerous situation when we see one coming and then act to save ourselves, or not?

The health of the home planet is our goal, and hard work towards that goal is the salvation of Humankind. If we can save the tree forests by growing more hemp instead, then let us do so. We shall receive a rich reward thereby, for the harvest gained can engender a success which must bring about further successes thru out the entire field of Human enterprise.

Now listen! Yes, listen and look and observe, and learn somewhat of new knowledge: *For thus we can surely see that a renewed and swelling growth of industrial hemp agriculture, along with the sending forth and building of Human colonies on Luna, the greening of Mars and the mining of the planet Mercury also, the efforts to establish a more efficient, faster and cleaner system of Human transport and to rebuild and heal Earth's major cities also, along with the drive to find a fuller understanding and control of nuclear reaction power and solar heat energy, the rejuvenation of landed agriculture and the farming of Earth's ocean, as well as the general cleaning and refurbishment of Earth thru massive Human effort and hard work is the wave of the future, a wave whose full cresting is not yet in sight.* And so we learn that there are, in fact, some least little things that we do know, and which might serve us now in these times of further need.

Tobacco Quittance

One very good aspect of hemp farming, an aspect which has been long awaited and is very much needed just now, is that this new crop will provide a better crop for tobacco growers to grow instead of tobacco. If there is one business on this planet which is a total waste of time and a violation of every rule of good sense and good health for the species also, it is the tobacco industry. Good riddance to bad rubbish, I say, and let those farmlands be used in better ways.

One would have to go far to find a stupider or more unpleasant Human habit than that of smoking cigarettes and fat cigars. The more quickly that this habit is broken by Humankind then the very much better off *Homo sapiens* will be, each and every one of us. Anything, including massive taxation and adverse legal judgments, as well as an enthusiastic education of the peoples, that can change the tobacco business into a new business would be good and beneficial for the race.

Many people, many good and decent people have been done unto death by the produce of these tobacco bosses, and only for the sake of mere money and transitory political power. Widespread bad health as well as the hateful pain of slow and ugly diseases have been caused by the encouragement and pimping of this Human weakness. As well, enormous and horrendous public medical expenses continue to become even more enormous and horrendous day after day, and with no end of those losses in sight.

Even worse, there is a guilty knowledge of Human frailty that is being demonstrated here, and has now been made quite clear to us all: That we are giving death to ourselves for sorry motives of greed that go beyond the wildest dreams of avarice and political gluttony, that we have shown a brutal, meat-eating disregard for the grief and pain that must be endured by the many cancered, blood sickened and heart attacked victims of the tobacco habit; and that those victims are individuals of the larger Family, our friends, neighbors and blood relatives who we should love as we love ourselves.

This certain knowledge of our own moral weakness has introduced a rancid, bitter awareness of Human corruption, and of biological treason itself, into the mind and soul of Humankind. This has brought the malignant growth of subconscience guilt within the spiritual integrity of *Homo sapiens*, and brings a sense of guilty failure into the living and breathing gathered family of the species entire. This is nothing else but species suicide, and a tobacco quittance from within the Human family shall be an affirmation of the Human desire to live forever and must, by itself, inspire a fresh enthusiasm for clean living and healthy growth for ourselves.

Let us imagine an occassion when you are enjoying a get-together with family members and friends. Some strangers come by with pieces of candy and other sweets, which they offer into the general celebration even though they know that these candies contain poisons. Later, when those who have eaten the poisoned candy have died from its ill effects, you learn that these strangers have benefited by being named as major beneficiaries in the dead people's wills.

These strangers might not have poisoned the candy but they knew that the poison was there. Also they knew that some of the poison, at least, would be eaten because they knew that the sweet candy was so tempting. Also they knew about the financial rewards that would come to them when the dead people's estates were divided among the heirs. Any local district attorney who heard about this situation would say that a prima facie case of premeditated murder for money has been established, and begin an immediate prosecution of those strangers for first degree homicide.

If it can be likewise established that these tobacco bosses knew beforehand that their product, nicotine, was both addictive and poisonous; and that they encouraged the widespread use of this product regardless of the inevitable deaths by grievous disease which must then surely occur; and that they profited enormously from the global sales of this product; then all the elements of a case for the premeditated mass murder and serious wounding by disease of at least one billion Human beings during the last 50 years or so will have been proved.

Ergo, the executive officers who head such corporations as The R.J. Reynolds Co., Brown & Williamson, The Lorillard Co., Liggett & Myers Tobacco Co., as well as the people who run the Philip Morris Companies can be prosecuted for massive crimes against humanity.

The largest and most powerful of these corporate entities is probably to be found at the main headquarters of Philip Morris. In general, it is best to attack and defeat one's strongest opponent first, so that when that opponent has been bested then the lesser opponents will fall back and give way. If the chief executives at Philip Morris can be successfully prosecuted for the premeditated murder of more than one billion Human beings, worldwide, during the last half century then Philip Morris will be destroyed as a viable business.

It is illegal for criminals to profit from their criminal enterprise. Upon conviction, therefore, all the assets of Philip Morris can be seized by the court. Any farmlands owned by Philip Morris can be distributed, either for free or at a very low cost per acre, to the various farmers who had been growing tobacco, and this will help them in their efforts to move away from tobacco and towards the growth of healthier cash crops. Also, as history has repeatedly shown, the redistribution of land is always good for the local economy.

The vast financial wealth which Philip Morris has looted and plundered while the rest of us have been dying from the cancers and other disease which they gave us may likewise be seized. Those millions upon millions of stolen dollars can be used to finance a massive program of medical research aimed specifically at finding a cure for cancer, at long last, as well as learning how to end sickle cell anemia, AIDS, and Alzheimer's disease.

O yes, indeed, sweet and sweeter and sweetest can be the uses of Human adversity! And if an American court cannot handle this job then let the prosecution be done by the World Court in le Hague.

That tobacco smoke causes cancers, blood circulation problems and premature heart attacks has long been well known, as legal evidence and scientific research have shown. Yet tobacco continues to be grown and its use encouraged. That this odious drug is also addictive to its victims has likewise been long known by the tobacco bosses. Yet even so, still tobacco continues to be grown and its use encouraged. Therefore, deliberate and premeditated mass murders of Human beings have been done here and continue to be done, even at the very moment of this writing. There has been fraud with malicious intention also done. Perjured testimony has been offered into evidence in dozens of courtrooms and in several national Parliaments also.

The perjured testimony was given in support of the malicious fraud; the malicious fraud has been done in protection of the deaths caused by the inevitable cancers and other health problems inherent in the wide-spread usage of tobacco products; and those millions upon millions of pre-meditated deaths have occurred as a direct result of the Human lust for gold and political power. Not even Nazis could have killed so many, and in such a short time as the last 50 years have been, and so devoid of Human compassion as these tobacco bosses have shown themselves to be. Thus do we see the ancient injunction, that "the love of money is the root of all evil," has again proved to be true, and with a very deadening effect upon the Human soul and upon financial profit as well, and this has produced as much of a dead-end situation as ever has been seen before in all the history of Human enterprise.

My God, and my God forever! These tobacco bosses are smart and sneaky and mean-spirited, the most wicked scoundrels alive on the face of the Earth today. The rest of us, addicted prisoners of their tobacco smoke and other false allures, have also been very foolish indeed.

This is the murder of ourselves by ourselves, the murder of individual Human beings by a crazed and warped economic policy of the species entire. The tobacco industry promotes, by necessity, a physical and spiritual wounding of Humankind, done by politically influential members of the Human family and to greater losses for everyone involved. The slick and sophisticated sales techniques used to sell tobacco products are nothing but gross and wicked lies told to unwary victims who are the children of our own kind, with both the persuasive liars and their victims being of the same peoples and everyone equally corrupted by the same process of public mendacity.

What kind of governments do we have on this planet, anyway, which allow and even encourage the massive poisoning and sickening unto death of their own populations? What manner of creatures are we, knowing as we do the poisons of tobacco smoke, that we continue to allow the tobacco industry to flourish and grow taller, and also allow ourselves to use those products of slow and addictive death?

We should have known better than this. And in fact, we do know better than this! Those senators, judges and lawyers who fail to help *Homo sapiens* as we struggle to cleanse this tobacco corruption from our presence shall themselves be impeached, condemned and removed from office. And, if bribery has occurred and been proved against them, then let those guilty senators, judges and lawyers be thrown into the hard prison of a durance most vile. This Human race shall not die now but shall struggle to live instead, and all efforts to the contrary shall be rebuked and quitted and washed away, so that a cleaner flower and fruit of Human maturation might then flourish in the fresh air of cleaner living.

If an individual Human being can break his or her habit of smoking cigarettes, then the whole Human race can do the same. When Humankind has expelled tobacco and tobacco products from daily usage, then by taking that one step alone we will find ourselves to be a finer, healthier species of living beings, and more self-disciplined, more fit to survive in whatever galactic community we might encounter out there in the darkness beyond Luna. Also, our personal living quarters as well as the planet itself will begin to smell sweeter and more spiritually alive. For the love of true Creation and for the true love of Human integrity as well, *Homo sapiens*, let us cease and desist from this addiction to the poisons of tobacco and tobacco economics!

Rain Forests, and the Churches

Our tropical rain forests are not to be damaged by Humankind, no matter what material wealth we think to find in there. Any persons who attack and plunder those forests shall be arrested by law and brought to trial for treason. Those rain forests are at the very heart of Earth's health. Any harm that has come to those forests due to the lust for gold and other wealth must be repaired forthwith and never repeated, and you can inscribe these words in letters of fire upon the deepest tissues of Human civilization, for that is just how true they are. In fact, and as a matter of law, if military forces must be called forth and used to protect those rain forests from Human greed, then let it be done.

Much forest lands in Central and South America and in Africa have been gouged away and despoiled, disemboweled and left belly-gutted unto a cruel ruination by the rampant mining of gold and other mineral deposits. Vast amounts of rain forest acreage have been butchered and chopped away, with the land left naked and bleeding raw, so as to provide grasslands and fodder for the pasturing and feeding of beef cattle. Thru out the Amazon river basin millions upon millions of trees have been cut down and left to rot on the ground so as to provide room for the growing of the coca plant, and this is done for the sake of making the narcotic pleasure drug, cocaine.

All of this is ludicrous! This is ludicrous in the extreme, a crazed warp of Human thought and a perversion of our natural tendencies towards territorial expansion. Yes, and I know that *Homo sapiens* is an immature and childish species, young and still growing. But does this mean, and is it strictly necessary or even desirable, that we should also be stupid as well?

What kinds of bargains are these? When we rob our homeworld of essential oxygen- and nitrogen-producing tropical rain forestation so as to rip more gold from the land, and so as to raise more cattle for the slaughterhouse, and to provide more cocaine pleasures for the vapid delight of the drugged lotus-eaters amongst us, and when the only planet known to be suitable for Human habitation is being severely damaged by such procedures and transactions then just how worthwhile are these bargains, anyway? How eagerly, and with what worthwhile purpose in mind, should the purchase of such bargains be sought? The survival of Humankind is the true profit we must seek here, and the safe health of our homeworld is likewise a goal to be sought.

This has been bank robbery on a grand scale. This is the plundering, not merely of money stolen from a bank, but the looting of our planet wherein the very life support system of Earth itself is the stolen treasure involved. No economic desires or any domestic political policies can ever justify a business practice so foolish as this.

What? Would you also subject yourself to a boring diet of bread and water just to save the expense of buying tastier food and drink? Because, to strip mine the rain forests in pursuit of gold and to lay waste those lands so as to make room for herds of beef cattle are net loss propositions of the very same type. Ultimately, in a negative profit situation such as this is, it is the robbers themselves who are finally robbed, as the properties being misused and consumed and thus lost forever are our own, *Homo sapiens*.

Are we a race of sapient beings or are we just a bunch of vandals and hooligans, now busily engaged in destroying the beauty of a system whose true beauty and wealth we do not yet comprehend? Is there any hope of Human maturity to be found within this generation of the species entire? Or, being caught in a pattern of juvenile delinquency wherein valuable things are destroyed and cast aside simply for the lure of adolescent thrills, for the adrenalin excitement caused by seeking after temporary wealth and the lust for transient political powers, must we now make our own homeworld barren and devoid of all hope for any natural and happy growth for ourselves and our posterity?

This is stupid in the Human head, that such a discussion should even be mentioned in the first place, or that such obvious advice must needs be given to a race of people who are even remotely aware of their own surroundings. What a bunch of dull knives we must be, and our minds so devoid of purpose, if we cannot cut more sharply than this. Must we also have detailed instructions as to precisely why it might be unwise for a person, naked and unaided, to go for a swim and a frolic in a river which is known to be infested with piranha fish and electric eels? Must we also read books of esoteric teachings so as to learn why one should not play games of hide-and-seek with a rogue bull elephant on the rampage, or why not to dive headlong into a live volcano while at the same time one hopes to keep a dinner engagement in the evening of that same day?

Why is it necessary to give such obvious advice to a species of beings who should know this much, at least, without being told? Even ordinary mice, unlettered and ignorant tho they may be, know enough to avoid the company of housecats, and with no formal warnings having been given to them. Is it not possible, then, that *Homo sapiens* should instinctively know that the massive wastage of Earth's forests in general, and of the tropical rain forests in particular, is likewise to be avoided?

How is it that everyone, apparently, knows of these problems and yet still these problems continue to remain unchallenged? Are committee meetings and public pronouncements which bemoan and otherwise deplore the slashing attacks being done against our own homeworld, and by ourselves, and for greedy economic gains, the very best and only shield we can offer against this threat of death to the Earth and the resultant threat of extinction of Humankind? Do we not yet understand that if we violate or disregard too many rules of natural law and order that the game must then be lost?

Where, oh where has the Catholic Church been nowadays? And what have all the Catholic bishops and priests been thinking and doing lately, as this constant pillage of Earth's natural resources continues unchecked and unhampered, day after day? The Catholic Church is the predominant spiritual influence thru out the nations of Central and South America. There is not one aspect of daily life, no political, economic or even military activity in those regions, which cannot be directly and powerfully affected should the Catholic church use its full weight either to stand against or in favor of any course of actions whatever.

Is it the considered opinion of the Catholic hierophancy, then, that the Catholic peoples of Central and South America should be so easily disenfranchised of their birthright by the commercial exploitation of their land, of their rain forests, and of their lakes and river waterways? Should the Churches stand idle and silent while these gross violations of natural law are being done, and to the greater loss for all Humankind? Of what good use is a great church, and of what benefit to Human civilization, if not to take action against such crimes and blunders as these?

The Catholic Church is one of the wealthiest and most influential organizations on the face of the Earth. The armies of the Vatican are vast and wide with countless battalions of unnumbered soldiers, and their generals can fight with invisible weapons, and to a great effect when the need is upon them. That need is here, and most definitely so. Armed and staffed and fully empowered, then perhaps the priesthood might remember that one of the most basic functions of the Catholic church is to offer sanctuary for the faithful during times of crisis. For here and now there is a strong need for sanctuary and protection, and not only for individual members of the church but for nations and even for whole continents of the planet as well.

These tropical rain forests must be preserved. This is a fundamental law of our own planetary ecology, and the enforcement of this law is a primal duty for any religious organization which hopes to claim responsibility for the spiritual welfare as well as for the physical survival of a peoples so endangered as *Homo sapiens* is today.

Jesus spoke, saying

"Lay not up for yourselves treasures upon Earth,
where moth and rust doth corrupt,
and where thieves break thru and steal:
But lay up for yourselves treasures in Heaven,
where neither moth or rust doth corrupt,
and where thieves do not break thru nor steal:
For where your treasure is,
there will your heart be also."
(Matthew 6:19-20)

Thus do we learn that there is and must be larger reasons for the existence of great churches, and for the Catholic church in particular, other than to gather fat wealth unto themselves. I mean to ask here, what is the use of all this fabulous wealth that has been taken and hoarded over the last 20 centuries, and what is the good of all the spiritual influence that has likewise been gathered and stored, if not to help the Human race during such times of great need as these are today?

The cleansing of Earth from the effects of industrial pollution and the remission of Human error in this regard must be a cause more holy and more essential to the salvation of all Humankind, and more devoutly to be sought, than any religious crusade or jihad has ever been since the written histories, both of nations and of churches, first began. During these days there can be no cause more righteous than this: That Earth shall be cleansed and saved so that Human dominion might continue to flourish on this planet, and hence Homo sapiens shall grow and expand and give light unto the dark void that awaits us beyond the conquest of Luna. Thus the will of Creation is to be fulfilled unto the final truth and fullest light of the Human soul unveiled, and that revelation shall be like the glory of pure fire.

And likewise with the Mormons, with the congregation of the Church of the Latter Day Saints: What should these people be doing right now? And what of the Hindus? And what of the Buddhists? And what of the faithful of the Hebrew, and of the peoples of Islam? Just exactly what are you people doing while the very ground whereon your churches are built is being contaminated, while the very air the preachers breathe as well as the food and water supplies of Earth are befouled and made filthy by the voracious rape of Earth's purity, and while the careless wastage of our natural resources continues to be done, and all due to the greed for money and for the love of opulent creature comforts and the lust for political power — just exactly what are you people doing in response to this question of Human fate?

And what of the Christians? They call for Jesus! They call for Jesus and for more of Jesus, and all for more salvation! The churches of Earth must do more than merely promulgate their own doctrines and gather more money for themselves while weeping over the sadness of it all, and while begging forgiveness from the eternal Maker of all things. Why not put your money where your mouth is? Great wealth and capital gains, aroused and enthused with religious fervor would bring most potent forces into active play on this question. An active, enthusiastic global effort, a great work accomplished by this whole generation of *Homo sapiens* as the species entire, is just exactly what we need to see and to do at this time.

The faithful must speak out. We must go to war, for we must be faithful to our own Creation. If the Human race should exterminate itself because of our own political carelessness and the economic greed of the privileged few among us, then all Human knowledge of Creation shall be ended. If the Catholics and the Mormons and the Protestants and the Jews and the Hindus and the Buddhists and those of Shinto and the people of Islam and the Christians and, for that matter, the Atheists also, cannot unite in this war against Human sin and weakness then the Human race must be foredoomed. As separate from each other as these churches have always been before this time, yet when we are now confronted by a dilemma of such an obviously worldwide import, then we should be able to stand united and together. Whether these people congregate in temples or synagogues or mosques or in churches or in open fields makes no difference, so long as we all understand ourselves to be dwelling in the midst of global danger, that our Human salvation lives and must always live within the Human soul, and resides therein for growth eternal.

And besides Central and South America, what of Africa? What of Indonesia? What of North America, Europe and Asia? What of Japan? What of Russia? Cannot the churches raise up their voices in those places wherein they now abide, and where they have abided for centuries and millennia up unto this day? Having been nurtured and cherished by the nations of Human civilization, it would be altogether fitting and most proper for the established churches of the world to employ all of their persuasive powers, those powers of spiritual guidance, of political influence and of financial resources, to help in this planetary housecleaning so as to repay and redeem all the favors of hospitality which they have always known and enjoyed up until now.

Oh, we can sing our religious hymns all day long, and we can ponder delightful sermons concerning the laws of Moses or the love of Jesus or the will of Allah or the wheel of Karma as often as might be desired, and we can utter prayers of hope and of Thanksgiving during every minute of every day. But let us not use these activities as a means whereby we might think to deny and escape from the very great task which now confronts us. Remember, as was written in the *Epistle of James*, 2:26, "For as the body without the spirit is dead, so faith without works is dead also." From this we should be able to understand that much of the current impassioned blather of religious fervor is so much verbal balderdash and nonsense, a panicked reaction of excess sound and fury, fanatic noise that signifies nothing and accomplishes nothing either, and represents a desire to hide from those very real problems and great dangers which truly threaten our continued growth as a living peoples.

For now there is much heavy work to be done. So much heavy work there is, in fact, that every man and woman of this generation needs to do hard work before there can be any hope of its full accomplishment. Now the species entire of *Homo sapiens* stands fresh, strong and newly poised at the edge of the dark void which awaits us beyond Luna, and with either doom or a shining triumph of life and divine light thence to be won. Shall we be stopped here, now and forever? Or shall we continue onward and skyward into this first millennium of Human adolescence?

All of these problems that we face can be solved with ease, when once we accept the truth that these problems do in fact exist and require responsive action. Thus it is the understanding that is all: For as the understanding cometh then all answers soon follow and all questions are soon solved, and Creation continues to unfold during the normal sequence of natural growth forever ongoing.

Trash and Garbage

By the way, what is the true meaning of all the trash and garbage that we now find thru out the countryside and in the cities, and which we stumble upon underfoot wherever we go? In every place a person might visit he or she sees more discarded refuse on the ground and in the streets, and why should this be so?

To our dismay we notice a veritable cornucopia of nastiness and filth all around us, and this sorry condition is most surely of our own making: Everyday we see the random scraps of paper on the ground, we see rags of dirty cloth and discarded junk metal, piles of excrement and other nasty wastes, bodies of dead and dying animals, slum neighborhoods which should be burned away and destroyed and then rebuilt to be clean again, fire-gutted houses with empty rooms and dark windows that face out upon an even darker night, and these bleak houses have secret passageways inside them that can lead to no goodness but only into hidden evils, as well as drunken whisky bottles and other broken glass in the gutters of the streets and on the sidewalks, rusted automobile carcasses, heaps of rotting food, stagnant pools of greasy liquids, and all this is done beneath a blue sky that is browned over by the stench and the smokes of industrial smog and, lo and behold! What kind of a garbage dump of Human vomit and petro-chemical wastes have we made of this Earth, anyway? Is this a planet where Human beings might dwell in healthy comfort, or has our world been made into a global pigsty where we Humans, like so many dumb boars and sows, roll about and frolic in the reek of our own defecations and other filthy wastes?

For lo and behold, and who has made our Earth into this slovenly mess of an open sewer? Because, this sloppy mess must have been made by a peoples who have not remembered to clean up after themselves or are too tired, too defeated, too lazy, or too unaware and careless to do so. This panorama of garbage which we see everywhere around us must surely help to sustain and feed the despair each of us feels inside his or her soul, a despair which has become so much an endemic part of all Human society nowadays.

Who, think ye, has caused this planet to look like a global wasteland? We have, *Homo sapiens*, and we must learn to live more cleanly than this. If we tolerate such a cluttering and such messiness in our personal surroundings then a messiness of thought and action must surely follow. This, in fact, is what has happened already. And anyone who does not believe that this is true needs only to wake up and look around, because the clear proofs of our degenerate condition are quite blatant.

The anti-littering laws must be among the strongest in the land. *For the sake of Human sanity and Human health, this is important for us to know and to always remember: Littering, now a minor offense which too many people feel free to ignore, must be made into a far more serious crime and with serious penalties involved.*

When you see trash and garbage all around you then inevitably, your own thoughts and actions must be adversely affected. Too much flotsam and jetsam floating in the water, for instance, is a certain sign that someone's big ship is sinking or has already sunk. Our own ship, this planet Earth, is in just such a danger today, and this is only because the childhood of the species entire has been so carefree and wanton up until now. In fact, if any thought had ever been given to community hygiene in the first place then we would not have this epidemic problem of global industrial pollution and other public effluvia, as well as this spreading stench of Human waste all over the planet, at this time.

As to the trash and garbage that naturally accumulates day by day, simply do as Earth itself does constantly: Recycle, recycle and recycle again, to reduce and reuse. Thus from discarded cloth you make new clothes, from junk and broken things make new goods, and from base metals you might even turn lead into gold if it may be done and you so will. Is not an ever-green pine tree, for instance, which is forever refreshed to drop new pine cones and is constantly made new again with greenness, and made from a mixture of earthly minerals and water which have been nourished by air and heated by the fire of sunlight, nothing else but a product of clean and eternal recycling? Is not all of life and of living but a constant process of making and remaking, of the eternal blending together in endless degree and fractions of proportion those eternal and most basic elements of fire, water, air and earth?

In all the vast and starry infinitude of the cosmos, besides fire, water, air and earth, and the spiritual grace of Creation, what else could there be of life? With this thought in mind we must recycle, recycle, and recycle again, so as to make better use of otherwise discarded matter and to clean this littered landscape of its gross and excessive rubbish.

Recycle, reduce and reuse when you can, and you then find natural and planetary needs, Human needs, waiting to be filled. Raw materials and natural resources are not meant to be merely used once and then simply cast aside or burned away, nor are they so plentiful as to be thus wasted and squandered without any thought of reclamation. *There is a potential here for a new business venture of Industrial Recycling, and there is a strong need that such a business effort be made.*

Industrial Recycling is a growth industry whose time has come, a growth industry of national and global importance wherein solid profits might be found, both real and of the Human soul, and for the general well being and betterment of the Human condition.

The Coming of the Glory

The problems caused by global industrial polluting are not mere nuisance issues raised by nitpicking do-gooders and bleeding-heart romantics, but are instead a cause for serious alarm and survival concern. Yet everything that has been done so far to make war against pollution has been done with difficult and hard won persuasions or thru courtroom battles waged by and against the various captains of industry. And this should not be so. Every Human being now alive, including the environmental extremists as well as the corporate executive officers, must now join hands and work together for the sake of the common struggle. Therefore, ergo and *ipso facto*, let this legal brouhaha of confused and public squabbling come to an end so that we can all get busy and do the great work, seeking to find the greater glory thereby.

Earth must be cleaned, a job for the whole body politic of *Homo sapiens*, and this is a simple fact of life. Therefore all industrial systems which cause pollution must be made clean or be cast aside and left behind, just as the big dinosaurs of ancient days were likewise cast aside, and that is another fact of life. The cleaning away of industrial pollution from our presence is not a useless burden to be shunned and avoided, but is instead an invitation into a period of growth and enrichment which is without precedent in Human history. The knowledge we gain in doing this work of planetary housecleaning will force us to develop talents and skills we would not otherwise have learned, and must revolutionize the Human condition beyond our wildest imaginings. By the time industrial pollution has been cleaned away we will no longer live in mutually opposed nations competing against each other on this one small planet, but as a united species able to seek our own way beyond this Earth and among the stars.

This is the real reason and full purport of all these many problems coming together at this time: That in seeking answers we shall find them, and that *Homo sapiens* shall be thrust forward and pushed into the age of species adolescence and on towards any age of adult maturity which is even further yet to come.

Thus let there be an end to public protests and other general demonstrations against resistant tycoon corporations. The demanding need of Human history, to always go onward and forward, requires that all such protests and resistance fade away and be replaced by a worldwide embracing of the global labor which now confronts *Homo sapiens*, an evolving species who is now involved and enthused by a crisis moment of forward motion. And after all, the basic question that has been asked of us is one of raw survival, and that is still another fact of life to be considered.

Indeed, why fight in the least little bit against the coming of the glory? For each and every one of us must know by now that we of *Homo sapiens* have been summoned, here and now, to do large works and busy labors for the furtherance of Human civilization. This generation of *Homo sapiens* as the species entire represents, in fact, the cutting edge of the Human knife thrusting into new levels of Human history which have not yet been fully found or made real.

We should also know that the efforts required for a successful cleansing of Earth are and must be, especially when one considers the expanding influence of Human history, even larger than the size of the planet itself. O, yes! The most certain potential for significant advance and achievement in the furtherance of our biological evolution, as well as for the historical education of *Homo sapiens*, is very much larger by far! These times and their needs are the budding movements of this Human race into its springtime growth of puberty, and thus must not be shunned and avoided but rather grasped into a full embrace instead, an embrace of species joy.

Yet they will not long endure, these days of wine and roses, for Human youth is fleeting and gone all too soon. So let us take the adventure, the wonder and the sheer adolescent thrill of it all for as long as we can, and gather our rosebuds while we may, and drink the fine wine and eat the good food also; for these are starry days of passionate splendor, of endeavors most fantastical, of magic journeys towards goals whereof we know nothing, nothing whatsoever, as yet.

Because more serious matters, matters of a Human adult significance, will begin to arouse our interest as a species sooner than we children can now know. Therefore I ask again: Why fight against the coming of the glory? Why fight against the coming of this best and most intense age of Human growth? Why not fully embrace the time of your greatest pleasures and further achievements? Why resist the naturally ordained entry of *Homo sapiens* into whatever galactic society there might be out there beyond the conquest of Luna, and thence into the galaxy beyond?

Puberty is a lot of fun, boys and girls! Surely we can imagine and believe that we are going to enjoy ourselves in a crescendo millennium of exuberant youth and most juicy pleasures, with the farthest reaching towards our most distant grasp of discovery and explorations thence to be found and fairly won also, and then fully enjoyed to the max, and then to go forward with the conscious knowledge that a fuller growth is always unfolding and moving onward both within us and around us as the maturing body of a species entire.

But there are problems here, and danger for the race as well, danger caused by this sudden rendezvous of Human ages. As we can see in the daily newspapers and hear from public gossip also, there have been severe tensions produced among us, worldwide. These tensions are similar to the heavy stresses naturally felt by any growing Human child who is forced and pushed into the previously unknown and unexpected puberty of adolescence.

But we are safe! We are safe, for so long as we take effort to save ourselves! Our dangers and fears are well known in the natural evolution of our own true Creation, my fellow children of Human desire, and we must not fall prey to these frenzied crimes of individual brutality and the waging of war among ourselves. Our fears are but a part of normal species maturation, and are to be resolved by our own conscious, deliberate efforts to go onward and skyward and highward from this present platform of the Human condition.

But we must try! We must make an effort! We must attempt to learn from the past and go forward from here with full knowledge endowed, if we hope to mature as an alive and growing species. We shall not be so ignorant as to repeat the mistakes of past experience; but we shall go forward with the lessons of Human history imbued within us and made one with the Human heart of hearts. Let us stop making savage wars among ourselves, and for stupid reasons also! Stop being the servants of Human fear, and stop killing each other, and lying to ourselves and to each other, and stop beating each other and torturing each other without mercy or without any sense of compassion, and stop being agents of death and desolation for all the other living things that grow around us!

Be humane, and be Human and be Human beings, and be the givers of light and of life! We shall love ourselves and each other, and we shall expand and grow into further territory, and we shall build perfect and most pure civilization, and we shall grow to be a species of gardeners, farmers, teachers, seekers of knowledge and makers of fire, and we shall help in the growth of the galactic soul when the time of our adult maturity comes round at last.

It is those same feelings of uncertainty and doubt, and the awareness of vague growth pains within the Human soul, that are now being experienced by the whole mind and body politic of *Homo sapiens*, and by each of us as individual boys and girls within the species entire. We are now involved, whether we know it or not, in the further maturation of our kind. It is to understand these quite normal fears of a dark and as yet unexplained future that we must now address ourselves. The basic understanding is all and everything; for when such an understanding cometh, then cometh also the glory and the light, and cometh also the making of the higher and most pure fire.

Digression

Recent events of bombing, and of other mayhem taking place even as these words are being written, must cause us to be afraid for the very survival of our kind and for the future health of this small planet. We see unresolved anger boiling over and into fanatic, global rage, so that the bomb explosion in Oklahoma City, US of A, seems to be just another small part of the larger pattern of fire and doom now being expressed and enacted thru out the whole of Human society. We must now be made aware of just who and what we are, as young children of Creation, before we destroy ourselves with the feverish passions of our inexperienced and, necessarily so, ignorant youth.

I am frankly amazed, for instance, to learn that so many of us seem to be so absolutely convinced as to the absolute truth of the various absolute causes for which so much absolute slaughter is being done by ourselves and to each other, and all with such an absolute certainty of mind and purpose. Let me say right now, that as a Human species and as individual Human animals within the species, we have gained absolute knowledge of almost nothing whatsoever. Of this, and of this alone, there is some reason to feel an absolute certainty of truth.

When everyone of us learns this much at least, that we are as yet but ignorant children struggling in the dark, that we are stumbling forward unawares and towards unknown goals, that these goals have been only vaguely and distantly glimpsed up until now by even the very best of the brightest thinkers and poets and daydreamers among us, and that all else is uncertainty, uncertainty and still more uncertainty, then and only then *Homo sapiens* will have learned a hard and good lesson well worth knowing.

Homo sapiens, do you hear me? Do we all see these words now written here? With our short history on a small planet that cannot even be seen by the naked eye from just a few million kilometers away from here, and most of us being less than two meters taller than a bug on the ground, and having barely left our home planet for the first time while knowing nothing of the galaxy around us, and so easily carried away by the rabid passions of the moment as we often are, and so easily moved into extreme patterns of mob behavior as we also often are, and so eager to justify horrible gore for the sake of what we imagine to be the higher goals involved, and being so utterly ignorant as we are of any life which might exist beyond this teeny-tiny world of our birth, we know next to nothing at all of any absolutes.

Tho we believe ourselves to be of an ancient lineage, wise and experienced in the ways of all living, yet so far as the stars in the void are concerned we are an adolescent species of 12-year old kids who have only recently been able to leave home for the first time and are now very much afraid of the unknown darkness out there beyond Luna.

So just exactly who do we think we are, to hurl death so freely among ourselves for the sake of religious and political beliefs which none of us fully understands, anyway? *Homo sapiens* has been walking erect and upright for about two million years or so, while the earliest examples of written language are less than four thousand years old, and the ruins of our oldest cities date back to less than six thousand years from today. At this level of Human growth, at this point in Human history, and when one considers the brief and short amount of recorded history involved, then just how much of real knowledge do we or could we actually possess? Not much, if the daily newspapers of the world are any indication, not very much at all.

This species has not even gone thru puberty yet, so how much real knowledge and how much real truth can we have possibly gained by now? The potential for fuller growth is certainly within the Human soul of each and everyone of our kind, however, or else why would *Homo sapiens* have even come into existence in the first place? The knowledge of truth and of the salvation of the Human soul always burns within us with a fire that is pure and clean, to shine forth when the final days have come. But for those days to come these days must first be saved; and it is to encourage the saving of these days that this book is written, to hope for the further-ance of Human education.

It would be better for we children of *Homo sapiens* to lay aside our absolute certainties about any political or religious or ethnic absolutes whatsoever, and to realize the full extent of our childish ignorance and youthful inexperience. Else our maddened passions must soon reduce this planet to a burned-out cinder and ourselves to so many chunks of greasy dead meat, and with even the hidden contents of our bowels turned into dust. We are like children rashly playing with fire. We think that we understand and control the fire, but we do not. Rather, it is the nuclear fire and the adrenalin lust to hurl that fire upon those within our own species whom we believe to be our foes but who are, if the fuller truth were only known, as confused and frightened as everyone else is, that threatens to control us. *Yes, this excited adrenalin lust to use the nuclear fire as a weapon of vengeance and conquest controls us, and threatens all of Human existence thereby, as when events are in the saddle and ride the soul of Humankind.*

Unless we behave ourselves as individuals and as nations and as a gath-ered Family, we might easily burn down the whole house and everyone within. What, O what then shall be the value and the worth of all our absolute truths, except as to demonstrate how absolute ignorance can bring an absolute failure to the species entire, as *Homo sapiens* extinct?

So let us take heed, boys and girls, and be warned. Be fully warned that despite your vanities and foolish pride you are not as strong and as smart and as wise as you think you are. *Homo sapiens* is not yet a finished, fully grown species of beings. There is still much to do and more to be learned before we can hope to achieve absolute certainty about anything.

Do Work, and Goeth Thou Forth

By the way, and to return to my original purpose, we should realize by now that the struggle to clean away the effect of industrial pollution and to thereby build for ourselves a better Technology is so massive and will require so much of a worldwide effort that there is no need to worry anymore about high rates of unemployment or economic inflation whatsoever. I SAY AGAIN: *That when <u>Homo sapiens</u> has begun the job of cleaning our homeworld then the political problems of unemployment and of economic inflation must vanish and be gone for quite a long time in the foreseeable future.*

The cleansing of an entire planet must surely provoke an economic resurgence, a situation wherein invention freely begets more invention, industry causing by itself further industry to be started anew or to be rebuilt, as the case may be, so that there is more than enough good work for everyone to do. Above all, this is not a time for idleness and stagnation. Rather, let us busy ourselves to clean our house so that we might enjoy a good hot supper and warm bed at the end of day.

Yes, ye children of Creation, there is much work for us to do. Sweep the floors and scrub the walls, wash the windows and make the beds, set the furniture back in place, make sure that the water supply is fresh and clean, then fix the roof and tend to the garden out back. Clean the stove and fix the plumbing. Let us just get busy! This is a housecleaning job, a cleaning of the globe, a cleaning of the Human condition, and a biological necessity of the Human life. Because there is such a need herein for movement and activity, because this general housecleaning must be a part of those larger actions which we see at work all around us, and we can also feel the need for these actions beginning to stir within us, then let the movement be started.

As we all know fully well, that to everything there is a season, a time to every purpose under the sun and upon the starry void. For instance, sexual lovemaking is not the only Human activity that naturally seeks a climax. Human history has its own moments of intense passion as well. Such a moment is now upon us, and we are caught inside the feverish, heated pressures of this moment, so that *Homo sapiens* must be close and very near to some great revelation of the Human soul.

The many wars of the last two thousand years, along with the various political, intellectual and moral schools of thought which have sprouted during the same time period like so many buds and leaves on a tree, as well as our incredible leaps forward in technological discovery are all aspects of the foreplay and the old in-out, in-out thrusts of Human history in motion. These fast and even frenzied in-out thrustings would indicate that whatever climax now approaches is sure to come as a real lollapalooza.

Our landing and walking upon Luna, and the subsequent efforts to move further abroad into the galactic house whose door is now unlocked and lies open before us is that selfsame lollapalooza, now coming round and made known to us at last. This event represents both a biological moment of decision and action in the young career of *Homo sapiens*, and is also an evolutionary leap forward in the growth of the species entire. This book is but a message of confirmation, written to inform the race that a climax of Human history is here to be won and that a whole new age of growth has come into being. It is just such a climax of history that, being larger than the planet itself, and the whole of this process is greater than the sum of all the various parts of Human history up until now, is exactly the type of a great lollapalooza that is needed here. For at this time and in such a situation, nothing less grand or less wide and high and as far-flung as this would serve to bring forth the birth.

These things to be done, tho large, are fully within the range of our Human powers. The need, that of raw survival, is the driving force which must enthuse and inspire our push towards the greatest efforts ever yet attempted by Humankind, and for the greatest goals. For these goals are those of life itself, of life seeking a renewal and rebirth of itself, the urgent urge of life reaching out to find more life, and of the Human light seeking a greater illumination.

The technological abilities are here, while the biological imperative for action is most clear and insistent, and is divine within the Human soul. All that has been so far lacking is the moral will to go forward, to clean this Earth as honestly as good boys and girls can do, and to reach boldly for the stars. This is the true coming of the ages, and the age of our adolescence has now begun.

Chapter II:

Morals

Evolution

As *Homo sapiens* has now come face to face with the darkness that surrounds and embraces our homeworld, and as we are eager to explore the void yet are also fearful of whatever dangers might be out there in the great unknown, it is most needful that we now learn more about just who and what we are, and of our social mores, and of the Human morality which must govern our behavior both as individuals and as the species entire.

The idea that there is such a process as evolution has aroused much religious controversy in recent years. In several bibles it has been written that Humankind was created in one day and has since existed, complete and unchanged during the passage of aeons, and that there has been no growth since the birth. We should know by now, however, that whenever traditional religious doctrine is contradicted by observable reality then either the doctrine or the reality has not been fully understood. Here, the observed reality is not false and cannot, therefore, be altered to fit our traditional beliefs. But rather it is we who must do the changing, *Homo sapiens*, as we come to a better understanding of these larger processes of history and biology with which we are so closely involved.

Evolution exists. Evolutionary growth can be demonstrated routinely in any competent laboratory, and can be observed in everyday life as well. Evolution is the very mind of Creation in eternal thought, the inward and outward breathing of the Creator's breath, and not merely a part of the design but the Grand Design itself, seeking fulfillment. Evolution, the advancing of the lower life forms into higher and more complex levels of existence thru natural selection, is the way Creation moves.

And it is not strange that this should be so. Indeed, how else could it be done? How else could there be any growth whatsoever, if there were no evolutionary process in consistent and universal work? Because evolution, and the natural growth resulting from normal maturation or from adaptation into changed circumstances, are one and the same.

For instance, we can see how a newly born infant soon grows into the mature and adult man or woman. We can also see that whatever knowledge and abilities the adult has gained, that then the next generation of offspring may safely assume that information as proven fact, and from that standing go onward to seek fresh additions. Thus every next generation of *Homo sapiens* must tend to go further forward than previous generations had gone before. The gaining of experience and knowledge is a cumulative process whose accumulations, by themselves, cause a greater momentum of evolutionary change to occur, and all in a continuity of history and toward the same natural goal of biological fulfillment.

A chunk of basic coal, having been compressed under heavy weight over aeons of time, and with high heat involved, gradually has the carbon squeezed away from its substance and is refined into a crystal of flawless diamond, cleansed and made pure by ordinary and everyday experience. Likewise, that *Homo sapiens* has now walked upon Luna and yet could not have even begun to do so two thousand years ago, nor could there have even been any thought of making the attempt to do so, nor could there have been any mechanical ability to do so, nor was there any realistic desire to do so, nor was there any pressing political, economic or military need to do so, and yet that deed had to be done and so was done in these days, is a certain proof that the force of evolution acts upon this species and that some growth, at least, has taken place. Quite clearly, then, a fundamental process of refinement is occurring here, thru out the whole mind and body of *Homo sapiens* as the species entire, and without any awareness on our part as to the evolving changes being done. Cruder and more base thought is being squeezed away from the Human mind by the massive weight of Human history and thru the normal maturation of our kind, so that we are involved in a process whose final growth towards our own condition of diamond perfection has not yet been fully understood.

Some people have said that Humankind has evolved from monkeys, and that at some point in time certain monkeys became *Homo sapiens*, and so here we are today. To account for the transition from monkey into Human they seek to find a "missing link", a crossover bridge wherein one species was somehow changed into another. There is no such missing link to be found, because there was no such transition in the first place. From the times of our most primitive beginnings until today, and for all of Human history yet to come *Homo sapiens* was, is and shall be *Homo sapiens*. What we have called evolution has been, in reality, the normal pattern of growth thru the various stages of Human development into fuller maturity. Let us not be offended because our anthropoid ancestors resembled apes. After all, everyone and everything has to start somewhere. We could not be where we are now had we not been there first, nor could we have grown as a species had there been no place to grow from.

And to me this is the great wonder of it all, that all of Human history has been growing towards this moment. That the species has evolved from its babyhood infancy, then into and thru the Human childhood, and that we have now taken the first step into our adolescent stage of growth is like rarest magic made real and solid, a divine grace having been given flesh and blood so that the will of the Creator has been done in ways that are still beyond our full comprehension, yet that will and those ways continue forever. The very size of the plan, the largess and the wild delicacy of it all, is enough to strike one dumb with both terror and delight. What other force but that of true Creation could perform such a sequence, and how else but thru evolutionary change could the grand movement be made?

AIDS Quarantine,
and Human Morality

Consider that the life cycle of the individual Human is repeated, in the galactic sense of species maturation, by the larger life history of the species entire. One consistent aspect of people's lives is that the girls tend to enter into puberty a little sooner than do the boys. This has always been true with individual Humans, and thus it must also be true with the species as a whole. This is why that movement which is known as Women's Liberation has come to such a widespread fruition at this particular time. That is the way it has always been with boys and girls individually, and that is the adolescent way it is with the species today.

As is always the case with youngsters whose adolescent glandular secretions have begun to make their presence felt, we find ourselves faced with fresh problems and new questions which must be answered and answered well. For instance, what shall we do about AIDS, *Homo sapiens*, this Acquired Immunity Deficiency Syndrome which has slain so many of Humankind already? This disease has the potential virulence either to wound the species severely or even to sweep this planet clean of all Human life, and so I ask again: What Do We Plan To Do Now?

This viral pestilence is of an unknown origin, is easily transmitted and is fatal to the degree of 100%. Neither any vaccine nor an effective cure has yet been found. What can be done to halt the spread of this plague?

So as to isolate the illness and slow down its progress thru the body of the species, the global quarantine of all AIDS carriers is essential. In fact, I am puzzled as to why such an obvious precaution has not already been taken. The medical research being done is useless, so long as the disease is allowed to multiply itself hourly, daily and weekly, month after month and year after year while the death toll continues to rise.

The most frequent method of spreading AIDS is thru sexual intercourse, both hetero- and homo-. But merely advocating the use of condoms during sexplay is not the guaranteed solution which is required. That is a band-aid remedy at best, a wishy-washy and namby-pamby attempt to avoid the drastic but necessary answer to this drastic and very deadly question. Special hospitals must be maintained for those who suffer from AIDS, so as to try and contain the thing lest it destroy us all.

But let there be no moans and groans here, no outraged protests over the loss of individual freedoms, because the very life of the species itself is herein under heavy threat. AIDS can and will do to Humankind what the Bubonic plague once did to the peoples of old Europe, but more thoroughly and with even a more rampant, random and epidemic death collection involved, unless some such measure as a global quarantine of the carriers is soon put into place and strictly enforced.

Insofar as personal freedoms and political rights are concerned, everyone can appreciate that the Human race as a gathered Family must have certain rights as well. Chief among them is our right to fight for our own survival. When a disease such as AIDS is on the loose and running freely within the species, completely fatal and so easily passed on as AIDS has proved to be, the species entire must either act to save itself or surrender, either fight for species survival or accept the possibilities of severe wounding or even of extinction.

Moreover, no one is thinking of punishing criminals here, but of curing or preventing a disease and the healing of its victims. Because AIDS communicates itself so easily from person to person and has a fatality rate of 100%, massive medical research combined with the legal registration, at least, or the quarantine of the AIDS carriers is the only answer possible which promises any hope of success in the struggle for good health. This is an extreme situation, a matter of life and death, and so only an extreme solution will suffice to serve the needs of this dilemma.

Let us remember, perforce, that this type of solution has certainly been used before now. The quarantine of epidemic diseases has been practiced by Human societies since before the first pyramids of Egypt were built, since before the first stone of the Great Wall was laid down. It is in these hospitals that the best medical research can be done, and it is the concentration of effort that provides any hope for the curing of this scourge. If the establishment of a global quarantine is without precedent in Human history, then so also without historical precedent is the arrival of a global epidemic which has so strongly aroused such a need in these times.

There is no peoples more in full need of taking a hard look at themselves and at their desperate situation, and at the alternative pathways that might lead them thru this quagmire of doubt and inner turmoil, than is this current generation of Humankind. Let us take note of our condition and of the threats involved, and then take the strong actions which are needed and necessary, and which are most consistent with the further easy flow of Human history. *There simply is no other answer possible but that this contagion of AIDS must be quarantined and curtailed from further spread.*

Further, while we are attending to the physical threat of AIDS, we might also remember the basic moral knowledge which has been taught unto Humankind since the very beginnings of Human thought and organized speech. With the widespread use of birth control devices, we seem to have released ourselves from the responsibilities of childbirth and parenthood. Thus we now feel ourselves free to toss all caution aside and to gratify whatever sexual desires that might serve to amuse us for the moment, and to seek the lust of hasty pleasures, and with no thought whatsoever for any future consequences. But with the coming of AIDS we must learn that such is not the case, and that these promiscuous sexual behaviors are not only stupid and greedy but may even be suicidal as well.

You shall not commit adultery, boys and girls. You shall not break that ancient law in the loose and easy manner which has become so much the common practice nowadays.

Today we can easily see that many Human beings, and we are members of a moral species, and we are fully aware that such ideas as Human morality do in fact exist, seemed to have forgotten some of the basic moral and civil laws by which the Human child has attempted to live for thousands of years. One of those laws, one of the Commandments of Moses, is that you shall not commit adultery nor suffer this random fornication to long endure within Human society. What? Did we think that Moses spoke in jest when he spoke thus? Were those words carved into tablets of granite stone so that we could then read them forever, just to satisfy some vague whim of puritanical law? Do we actually believe in our heart of hearts as individual beings, or as a nation or even as a whole planet of peoples, that we can ignore this most ancient law and then suffer no grief in repayment for the broken trust involved?

YOU SHALL NOT COMMIT ADULTERY, you boys and girls of *Homo sapiens*. That law is ancient and simple, and should make good sense to Humankind by now. Just let us look around at ourselves, *Homo sapiens*, and see how the essential love and bonding between man and woman as the husband and wife of the race is being so casually mocked, ignored, and otherwise disregarded during these times of species turmoil and commotion. We must also know that such a time of turmoil, and these many and heavy turmoils are most normal to the ongoing process of animal growth, must surely be intensified when a younger age of Human maturation is shoved and pushed into a higher level of development.

Just observe the boredom and the doubt which now plague so many of us, and which are revealed on the faces we see everyday around us, and which a person might also see on his or her own face looking back from a glance into a smooth mirror, and note the exhausted, dead fatigue with life itself which is thereupon revealed. Each and everyone of us must look at ourselves and at each other to see what we have done to Human hope, and which we continue to do even at this moment of writing with our manic flouting and breakage of this ancient rule. You shall not commit adultery, boys and girls, and this morality involves not only the struggle between sacred and profane love but is also essential to the biological health and moral stability of the species entire.

Just as our sexual organs are placed at the center of the Human body then so also must our sexual behaviors be at the very center of Human society and social mores, and are at the center of each person's personal health also, and must be at the center of each person's moral integrity as a living Human being. However it is that a man or woman behaves at the center of his or her body is and must be likewise central and essential to the health and spiritual truth of the Human soul, of who a person truly is, and of who the man or woman truly wishes to be.

Here, while we are living with the many stresses caused by overpopulation and with the latent fears of a nuclear bombardment laid heavily upon us, and this is all in a world where our food, water and air supplies have been thoroughly contaminated by industrial pollutants, and as we are also much afraid of the wall of darkness that lies beyond our first steps newly walked upon Luna, we are doing sexual adulteries everyday and in every which way that next occurs to our bored, jaded and terrified minds. Beef cattle in a slaughterhouse, knowing yet not fully understanding the approach of their bovine doom, behave in the same frenzied manner of sexual excess as we Human beings are doing today.

And, we are going out of control in our everyday living because of this. We are losing our moral balance, both as individual persons and as a race of creative beings, and when we lose our moral balance we lose everything. For instance, let us look at the American singer named Madonna Louise Veronica Ciccone, as she performs an impersonation of the Eternal Whore who always appears whenever great nations are falling into corruption and decay. Then let us further take note of our own reactions to the style and substance of her life.

Two thousand years ago there was another Madonna, the Mary who is remembered for her virgin purity and for the divine nature of her immaculate conception. Now we see this new Madonna, a girl who sings and dances before us as a wilted flower of fallen virtue. Yet we appear to love and admire her fallen virtue while giving no remembrance to any thought of ideal purity, perhaps because that ancient thought is only dimly remembered by ourselves nowadays. Ergo, as when sheep are led to the slaughter by a Judas goat, we are ourselves being led into a dead-end street of degradation and loveless sex as we follow the wanton example shown by the public and most lewd performance of this carefree, fancy dancer and those of her ilk.

And just see how empty and utterly without value all life now seems to have become during these times of loose behaviors and abandonment of all sexual morals. We can easily see how, in the end, that we are left with nothing but the empty memory of pleasures which were false in the beginning, done more so as to scratch an itch of sexual frustration and to relieve boredom rather than to provide any true refreshment or sense of renewal for the Human soul. For this is truth: That just as you behave at the center of your body then so also, for good or for bad, is the central truth of your own Human soul revealed and fully expressed.

We have applauded this new Madonna, and with a wild, feverish lust of public approval that begins to resemble the adoration of religious worship. What is wrong with us, *Homo sapiens*, that we should react in this way? Have we lost all our wits? Is there no rag of sense left in Human thought? Can we not recognize a lost and sad child when we see one, and a very flagrant whore as well, especially when she parades her easy and most naked ways right before our fully opened but unaware eyes? Have we no sense, at long last, of the choice between good and evil, or even that such a choice exists in the first place?

Those people who died during the bumbling and stumbling fall of the glory that had once been the Roman Empire must have seen many public performers such as she. Because, performing lewdly and with a frenzied abandonment of all traditional moral virtue, and thereby encouraging all the onlookers to follow the example of her own loose behaviors, she encourages the immoral efforts towards our own years of decline and Roman Empire collapse. Bewildered and confused by our fears of an uncertain future sexually, we are following the same path of wine-drunk, besotted behavior that was once walked by those dying Romans and, I have no doubt whatsoever, towards the same conditions of loss and final despair.

We must know that this behavior, this frantic search for sex, sex and more raw sex, sex done for the sake of cheap thrills and easy pleasures, is the central destroyer of any true love between man and woman. The groin is at the center of the Human body, and if we cannot be honest therein then we cannot be honest in any way, neither with anyone else nor with our own selves as individuals, nor in any other normal Human situations whatsoever.

If there is no sense of right and wrong in Human sexual behavior then that lack must affect all other aspects of Human society. There are only two sexes herein involved, boys and girls, and we shall be Man and Woman of the species entire. If these two of Humankind cannot be honest with each other then how can there be any honesty at all, in any place of Human conduct or in any situation?

We must decide now, ye sons and daughters of Humankind: *do we seek to be a species of male and female whores, liars, thieves, and murderers of each other, or shall we aspire towards the ideals of truth and the beauty of the Human soul which have been spoken of and promised by the prophets and elder teachers of our race?*

These two Madonnas, coming as they do at the beginning and at this nadir point of the Christian era, make for a significant set of parenthesis marks, marking and defining the punctuation of passing millennia. When Christianity was young and fresh there was a more clear sense of the beauty and the truth of it all, and so the Virgin Madonna was the Lady of the day. Now, philosophically frustrated and disappointed by two thousand years of constant war, and also faced with apparently hopeless fears of a dark and unknown future, we greet the fallen Madonna as a symbol of our own loss of hope.

As when a long distance runner who was eager and vigorous when the race first began is most weary at the finish line, then just so does the spiritually exhausted sexgirl now come to sing and dance among us where the Virgin Madonna had once stood before. That the model of virgin purity has been replaced by this new Madonna of excess and folly and vanity is, and must be, a clear and certain sign that a great cycle of Human history has now traveled full circle. Thus do we see one age of the World passing away even as a new age of Human thought and endeavor comes into view.

Darkness and Light

What are the reasons for this global breakdown of Human morality, and why has this decline of public morals become so prolific, and why does it happen at this particular moment of our history? At least part of the problem is caused by the pressures of overpopulation. As Humankind is now crowded together more closely than ever before, packed against each other more tightly and bumping against each other more frequently, it is only natural that extreme behavior patterns should begin to emerge and even to seem normal.

But *Homo sapiens* has now landed upon Luna, and in so doing we have entered a hitherto unexplored territory wherein the possibilities for species growth and expansion are virtually without limit. The mere knowledge that such a breakthrough has occurred, that there is more than enough room for the further spread of our Human family, that there can be other places to live besides this one planet and that there is a light at the end of the tunnel, should help to relieve some of these overpopulation pressures. *The certain knowledge that there is a possible solution to the problem must, by itself, help to ease the grosser tensions that the problem has caused.*

However, this entry into unknown and therefore possibly hostile territory has further produced even more anxieties and fears within the species. We see signs of fear and panic reactions to the fear, acts of individual and national madness, widespread drug addiction and chronic drunkenness, random and frequent acts of rabid brute viciousness, the breaking up of family relationships and the apparent loss of love between man and woman, the decline and the collapse of national economies, the popularity of bizarre religious cults, and all helping to produce a claustrophobic atmosphere of bewilderment, frustration and fanatic rage which carries with it the threat of war, war, war and even more war within the species entire.

Every one of us is running wild, and we are running wild against ourselves as members of the gathered Family. Criminal deeds have become commonplace and without conscience, without any sense of right and wrong. Liars and lying have become the rule rather than the exception in Human conversation. Murders are done everywhere and at all times of day or night so that the species seems to be killing itself, individual by individual. True love declines and is replaced by raw sex, so that romantic lovemaking happens from mere force of habit rather than from the true desire of life to procreate and reaffirm itself. Insanity and brutality are as rampant within the Human populace as are the frenzied actions of a pack of hungry dogs let loose to run wild thru a meatpacking slaughterhouse.

Such global trends do not occur by chance. There must be a reason which justifies and compels such a species-wide behavior pattern as this; and that reason must be, and this is necessarily so, one that is wide enough and large enough to touch upon the whole mind and body politic of Humankind. Thus we must ask ourselves this question: Has there been any recent event of Human history that might indeed be that large, and which might have cut deeply enough into Human awareness so as to account for the complete social and political disorientation whose full effects we are experiencing nowadays, and to the subconscious doubt and shocked confusion of every man and woman of the gathered Family?

Let us begin to think of the species entire as a larger and greater living creature, a growing entity named *Homo sapiens* whose greater mind and body is made from the lives of many upon many of male and female Human beings, and that each one of us is a cell of that body, and that we now seek to live and go forth from this cradle of Earth, and then ask such a question in this way: When a person comes home late at night into a dark house, what is the very first thing he or she tries to do? And when you find yourself to be in a dark room, what is your own first thought of action?

As a normal Human being, your very first thought here is to find and tippy-tap the light switch, to build a fire in the nighttime forest, to make a light which will banish the darkness of the ancient cave.

This is a normal Human reaction to darkness, a routine and natural reaction from a species which is predominantly visually oriented. Because we cannot see very well in the dark, my fellow children of *Homo sapiens*, darkness makes us nervous and afraid. This is not a matter of cowardice but is a survival technique, a defensive mechanism which we all share. It is this very need, the desire to find or make a light from within the darkness that surrounds us, that shall be the truth and the growth and the fullest light of the Human child. The knowledge that the light exists, and even in the seeking of the light, shall be the salvation of the Human soul.

Thus when we consider the previous question we must remember that we of Humankind are newly landed on the moon, that for the first time in Human history we have set foot upon a planetary body other than Earth, and that this deed has changed everything in ways we do not yet understand. ***When the first man walked upon Luna he entered, in the name of Homo sapiens, a dark room.*** That feat of those first feet, that entry into a dark, silent and apparently empty house, that first step into the unknown is the subconscious cause of the terror which has produced such crazed and warped behaviors as we have seen and done, worldwide, during these recent years. *Homo sapiens,* as an evolving species of potentially sapient and creative beings, is afraid of the dark. Because we are afraid of the dark, we have been afraid to grow and expand into a darkness wherein no light but the far distant stars in the void has yet been seen. ***The writing of The Coming of the Ages is the moment when the species entire of Homo sapiens has reached out to find and tippy-tap the light switch, to turn back this night of our confusions and make bright the glad day.***

Thus, in effect and in reality also, we are retreating into species suicide rather than going forth to seek our natural destiny. In spite of all our bombast and clever skills we are what I have said unto thee up until now: That as a young species, young and unfinished in our growth as we most surely are, we are like a bunch of 12-year old boys and girls who have recently left home for the very first time, and who are now puzzled to the point of a near panic unto global madness by the very newness of it all. Rather than accepting and seeking the outward, upward growth now needed we are attacking inwards, attacking each other, and in full attack upon ourselves and against our own best interests thereby.

We, the growing boys and girls of the Human childhood, have been and still are afraid of the dark, and our landing upon Luna has produced the anxiety which is the true cause for all the chaos of uncertainty which we now see around us and also feel within our personal selves. Thus this chaos of global madness comes from our nervous fears and youthful inexperience rather than from any conscious desire to do evil. *I must say again, that this chaos of global madness comes from our nervous fears and youthful inexperience rather than from any conscious desire to do evil or to harm ourselves.* There are very few truly evil people here, but there are many frightened children now present who are acting out their fears.

As when a stone is dropped into a calm lake of clear water, sending out ripples from the center of its splashdown impact, then just so has that one small step upon Luna produced global ripples of shock thru out the whole realm of Human awareness. Tho we might not have mentioned these fears amongst ourselves, these fears of the unknown, yet everyone knows or feels that we have reached the limits of our growth upon this planet. Everyone senses that something, something, something new and very big is on the move and fast approaching.

Therefore the question, whether spoken aloud or only vaguely sensed, is this: Where do we go from here? And further: What do we do now and how to begin, and why?

Even tho we feel the need to grow we have not yet realized the direction of the growing, and so we are turning our aggressive drives back against each other, against ourselves. It is as if an unhatched eagle, not yet understanding the process of hatching and with no knowledge of the blue skies and high clouds and gusty headwinds soon to be flown, were to peck savagely at its own breast instead of against the inside of its eggshell enclosure. For that is exactly what we are doing right now, *Homo sapiens*. We are fighting amongst ourselves, in a frightened avoidance of any outward growth and expansion from this egg of Earth.

We have heard that "Where there is no vision the people perish." Those words, written elsewhere and in other times, apply today with massive force. As a species we have filled this planet to the point of overpopulation. We have climbed the tallest mountains and plumbed the deepest oceans. So far as physical achievement is concerned, what else is there left for us to do here?

True, we must cleanse the Earth from the poisons of industrial pollution and we must come to a finer understanding of the ideals of Human technology, but what comes next? Where do we go from here? Where is the destiny, where is the sense of any purpose, of any goals to be sought? Where is there any vision of Human history, of growth and of the fulfillment of that growth? Until this day no one has known, and it is the lack of that knowledge which now confronts us and has robbed Human life of all its true meaning.

So it is indeed true, and we can feel that truth within each of us and see it now expressed around us, that where there is no vision the people perish. Yet I say unto thee here and now that the opposite is just as true: That where there is a vision, where vision has been restored and the eternal light is seen again, the people will then live to strive and struggle with a renewed vigor fully refreshed, in achievement of that vision.

Children in school must learn their current lessons before they can pass into higher levels of education. So it must also be with *Homo sapiens*. There are lessons to be learned now and knowledge to be gained which will serve us well in days to come, so that Humankind can move into species adolescence. We are not children anymore. We are now growing towards the Human adulthood. But we are still young, very young and inexperienced, still possessed of some basic innocence, at least. The Human child must mature, because a time of great growth is here and now upon the mind of the species entire. Many of our most firmly held beliefs must be left behind as new thoughts begin to emerge, as greater insight into the Human condition is realized.

Yet do not fear, my fellow children of Human desire. There is much to be learned during this passage from old ways of thinking into the newer and fresher paths. This learning of new knowledge and the acceptance of greater truths will not be easy. We must have learned from Human history by now, however, that nothing right and good has ever been easy to do. The words written herein might arouse anger from within the deepest soul of *Homo sapiens*. That anger is based on fear, fear of the unknown, fear of the dark. But let us not be afraid, *Homo sapiens*, for our growth is fully within the vision of the divine Will. Our movement towards the fulfillment of that Will is known and shall be accomplished to the fullest degree when the final days have come. Even I, the writer of these words, am totally blind. Yet with darkness as my constant companion I still know and shall know forever that the light is there, to be sought and to be seen.

Blood Relations Within the Gathered Family

Is it true that as one grows older, that then one always becomes wiser as well? So far as individual persons are concerned we see that this is not every time the case. But in certain areas of thought, and where the whole Human family is concerned, with its own survival and spiritual well-being, it must be necessarily so. Racist hate and fear within the Human race is one such area of thought wherein wisdom must be made to follow along with the coming of age.

The growth towards species maturity involves, and must involve, the learning from the mistakes of Human history so as to become more experienced as a species, more fit for survival and less vulnerable to the threat of biological civil war within the Family. Human maturity and species awareness also involves growing up and away from racist thoughts and actions which have produced only fear and misery, anxiety tensions of racial guilt, and social disorder thru out all the centuries of recorded time. Some wisdom, at least, must surely come as we abandon and grow beyond these doctrines which have always triggered an overflow of adrenalin, but which have also given us only war and more damage to Human society. This is especially true when we see nothing but cheap thrills, dead Human bodies and wasted passions to show for all the pain caused.

Homo sapiens has now walked upon Luna. That event changes everything. By expanding our horizon of growth, Humankind has thus gained a vantage point from which to look back upon Earth and at our own history here. From that vantage point we can see that many of the racial conflicts within the species have been just plain silly, and all the sadder and more dangerous for that very silliness. There are a few false assumptions which have led to false beliefs within the Human community. Those assumptions must now be cleared away just as rampant foliage must be cleared before a new house is built here, so that a fresh understanding of the Human condition may be found.

One of these is that Human beings have white, black, or yellow skin colorations, and this is just not true. The visual evidence before each of us says so, quite clearly and as a matter of naked fact: That every one of us is brown, Human Brown. Lighter or darker brown as the case may be, but each and every person has Human Brown skin nonetheless.

This perception is not a minor issue of wordplay but is of crucial significance. As long as we continue to perceive ourselves as having different skin colors, we will also see ourselves as belonging to mutually opposed racial groups. Thus we must learn, and we must know this to be true: That the Negroids are not as black as coal nor are the Caucasians as white as snow nor are the Mongoloids as yellow as lemons are, but that every individual being of *Homo sapiens* is brown, and that Human Brown is the color of all this Human flesh. There are no people of this species who are not without the color of their skin. Thus everyone now alive is a person of color. That color is brown, Human Brown, for Human Brown is everywhere upon the face of the Human soul.

Moreover, there are not several races of Human beings on this planet. Rather there are various peoples of the Human race, members of the Human family. We hear talk about harmony between the races, of racial equality, and of racial toleration, and all that talk is just sheer folly and nonsense. The Mongoloids, the Semites, the Negroids and the Caucasians are not separate races. We must stop believing that the species has been so created. This knowledge, that all Human beings are fleshed in shades of brown skin, that there is but one race of Humankind on this Earth, must be learned and embraced thru out the whole realm of Human society. Human blood is Human blood. That is a biological fact of life, just as all Human flesh is Human flesh.

Therefore all these people who have been verbally abused, physically assaulted, murdered, beaten, tortured, robbed and insulted with such racial slurs as honkys, niggers, chinks, and kikes, are you, *Homo sapiens*. Yes, these micks, krauts, wops, dagoes, gooks, spicks, gringos, Mexican greasers and Japanese nips are us, *Homo sapiens*, and us alone. Who else do we think is on this planet, anyway, besides ourselves and the rest of animal, mineral and vegetable Creation? There are no separate races involved in this question, but only the Human family of *Homo sapiens* is here and in place. We need to recognize ourselves as ourselves, the species entire of Humankind.

Yes, we have met these people many times before and we know them quite well, because they are ourselves. When we attack each other for such racist reasons we are attacking the Human race itself, of which each of us is a member. Rather than degrading ourselves by degrading each other we shall glory in the potential for redemption that burns with eternal fire within each Human soul, and celebrate the variety of Humankind. Any vicious arguments and ugly actions caused by the provocation of minor racial distinctions within ourselves, is treason against our Family of *Homo sapiens*. This must be voided from the Human soul in the same way that tainted or unclean food is vomited from a person's belly.

We must understand that when we try to push down our fellow Humans we are, by that very act, holding each other and ourselves back. Think of the species as being like a vast army whose soldiers are working towards a single goal, a team of athletes trying to win a victory, a complete organism that can be successful only when all its various members work together. Thus each Human being has a vested interest in the success of the species and likewise does the species have an interest in the success, happiness, and good health of each of its members.

John Donne, the English writer, once observed that "No man is an island, entire of itself; every man is a piece of the continent, a part of the main; if a clod be washed away by the sea, Europe is the less, as well as if a promontory were, as well as if a manor of thy friends' or of thine own were; any man's death diminishes me, because I am involved in mankind; and therefore never send to know for whom the bell tolls; it tolls for thee." This is a fairly clear statement of a solid fact of biological truth: That there is a large entity in residence here, whose name is *Homo sapiens*, and that each man or woman of us is an individual cell of that greater being. Ergo, racist hatred within the body of the species entire is not merely unpleasant and distasteful, but represents an actual cancer of biological treason within the real body of the gathered Human family.

For we must learn that there is no question here of racial toleration within the body of *Homo sapiens*, because there are no separate races involved. What we need instead is to know a racial recognition of the species entire, a knowledge learned from within our myriad population of Human Browns. There must be an acknowledgment of the species entire that is known and felt by all the various people who are made from the basic elements of fire, water, air and earth. By Creation we are inspired to seek the fulfillment of our potential for growth and fullest blooming. For just so has each of us been made, and is made, and shall always be made. *Homo sapiens* is a child of Creation, a blending of dust and water that has been nourished along by the presence of air and fire, an inspired mixture which is common to the making of all existing substance.

There are not and never have been any separate races who must some-how struggle towards a mutual toleration of each other, despite what we might have thought up until now. Rather there is and always has been only one race of Human beings, one species of *Homo sapiens*, one Human family, a family with many upon many of diverse and various children. A happy toleration between mutually opposed racial groups is, at this stage of Human development, an impossible goal to achieve.

Yes, you can sing your love songs and write poetry and orate eloquent sermons of passionate truths for as long as you care to do so, yet always will that goal of happy toleration between mutually opposed groups elude you, Homo sapiens. Much easier to find is tranquility within a species which recognizes itself as a whole body. When we recognize that each one of us, by virtue of the biology and the common history shared by everyone now alive, is a member of the same kind and a child of the same family, then *Homo sapiens* will have taken a significant step towards species maturity.

Those people who refuse to recognize the species entire will always continue to urge those same racial, religious and political tensions which have brought war, ruin and grief to every Human civilization that has yet arisen upon this planet. Therefore, *Homo sapiens* must make a conscious and deliberate effort to educate itself concerning the many and varied aspects of the Human condition. *There comes a time when this constant destruction of one civilization after another, and merely because the Human children of Creation cannot recognize their common Humanity, must come to an end so that further Human growth may occur.* That time has arrived and is here now. You shall learn to love thy neighbor as thyself because, in truth, you and your neighbor are one and the same as each other, each involved in all Humankind.

As maturing boys and girls of *Homo sapiens* we should realize that as we now stand poised before the darkness of the void, we stand alone. Of course, the love of true Creation is a gift of wonder and power that awaits us beyond the brightly lit full moon of Luna; but then again, the Lord helps those who help themselves. Except for each other, there is no one else to help us if and when any help is needed. Thus it follows that if we stand alone, *Homo sapiens*, we must also stand together. Each of us comes from the same place, we each spring from the same source of Creation and inspired mud. We each share in the common history of the species entire. All of Humankind have shared in the normal turmoil and travail of species childhood, and we have all grown together towards the dawning of this new day, this first small step walked upon Luna which is itself a giant leap forward in the Human mind.

You are all of the same kind, *Homo sapiens*. And thru out this vast and unknown universe there are but a few things that are sacred to you and to yours alone, such as the touch of Human flesh to Human flesh, the knowledge of Human blood as Human blood and the awareness of the Human soul that moves us, each and every one.

Man or woman, it makes no difference. We are as one, joined together beyond any unjoining, tied together beyond any untying or breaking of the knot, fused at the groin of man and woman. No matter how light or dark brown your skin might be, Human Brown is still your color. There is no romantic dreaminess here, but rather a hardcore statement of animal biology: That a Human being is a Human being is a Human being is a Human being, and has been given the potential for further growth towards greater fruition and maturity. So now let us get busy and grow up, and let us now stop this childish name calling against each other, so that we can go forth from Luna and carry our light into the darkness beyond.

Yet I know full well that in spite of all the books written and the fine speeches made in the past we will, *Homo sapiens*, continue to embrace these racist and anti-Human thoughts and deeds for so long as racial distinctions between various peoples remain. But I also know that there must be unity and harmony within Humankind, and that a species whose members fear and then despise each other cannot survive among the stars, so that any potential cause for internal species warfare must be overcome, suppressed, rechannelled and left behind.

Racial prejudices die hard. Such untruths, even after their falseness has been clearly proved will often continue to flourish anyway, disregarding any sense of right and wrong and in defiance of all logic. They are like maggots in the brain; maggots that not even fire can always destroy. For such reasons we must deliberately seek to change ourselves as a species. We must, young and emerging adolescents as we now are, make a conscious and purposeful movement towards the Human adulthood.

Thus let there be an active, vital and deliberate mixing together and intermingling done within the gathered family of *Homo sapiens*, made to occur vast and wide thru out the body of the species entire. Just as there is a natural movement of climate from one season into another and thence to another, and all being done for reasons of health and for the continuing prosperity of all things living, there shall be a biological mixing together done within Humankind. A worldwide encouragement of love, marriage and childbirth between Caucasian, Negroid, Mongoloid, and Semite men and women, the rebirth of the Human child into fresh growth, is now in order just as the natural progression of seasonal change is always in order and endures forever.

Let there be a blending and mixing together of the various peoples, a male and female blending thru out the race that is not merely tolerated but is admired and approved as a goal to be won, a barrier to be broken and with fuller freedom gained, and the ending of these internal tensions which have damaged us as a species so severely in the past. Yes, let there be a mingling of Human flesh and blood with Human flesh and blood, and Human children born into the new age thereby. Thus the smaller groups can multiply into the larger group of the Humanoid family, into the living species entire, and with a vast increase in the powers of Human intellect, strength, and talent achieved and newly found. Only in this way of total racial intermingling can the pure Human begin to emerge and eventually mature into species adulthood.

We cannot continue to exist as a species for much longer, fractured and splintered and mutually hateful to each other as we now are. As to who has been right or wrong in the past is of no importance whatsoever, except in that some truths of moral knowledge must have been absorbed into our Human awareness by now, and we must also absorb this idea: That the virtues and the many vices of the Human childhood have been shared and done by us all.

There is just no good sense in throwing curses or casting blame upon other people for past or present wrongs, because other than *Homo sapiens* there are no people here. During the age of the Human childhood we have all been brutal and stupid towards each other from time to time, and this has been due more to our own childish ignorance and inexperience more than to any deliberate desires to do evil and be wicked. There is no one else at home here but us Humans, not now or ever before. Thus this is most true, that it has been we and we Humans only who have been our own heroes and also our own worst villains as well.

These hot and angry passions which are beginning to carry us towards the nuclear fire, along with the poison gas victims and other random dead meats of Human slaughtering that are sure to come with whatever major war is next in preparation, and for whatever political or religious or racial causes which we imagine to be true, are instead terribly false and terribly wrong at this time. We have made these wars before, *Homo sapiens*, and we might have learned to do better and be wiser by now. As growing children we must either continue to learn as we mature or, and if we do not, we shall die young and unknown and unloved, as *Homo sapiens* extinct.

It matters not what I as an individual Human being do or do not believe to be true. My own personal preference as to right or wrong is of no consequence at all, for this is a thing of the species and of species maturation. We must make this move towards racial union, a movement of the Human mind and soul, for no other reason than that the time has come for us to do so. As when a flock of birds, feeling the colder air of winter approaching and sensing a shortage of both food and physical comfort decides to fly south for the winter, and not just because one bird begins to fly wild but because all the birds know that they must now seek a warmer climate, then just so must we Humans now leave those small prejudices behind and join ourselves together in common effort towards the finding of larger knowledge, to seek the moral and biological union within the gathered family of Humankind.

Homogenize yourself, *Homo sapiens*, homogenize the body of the species entire so that the source of so many past problems will simply fade from existence, leaving us free to go on from here with less troubled thought in mind. For we are of a kind. We are the blood related children of the whole Family, the Human expression wherein the eternal will of Creation seeks to fulfill itself, and each one of us is an agent of that Will.

Just think of the infusion of fresh blood poured from all peoples of the species into a more freely flowing genetic pool, and of the surge of biological growth which must surely result thru the remixing and reblending of Human genetics from within the race. We can change ourselves, we can remake *Homo sapiens* into a new race of Humankind, born from the old but stronger and smarter and healthier than we have been so far. When we see that there are no more of what we perceive to be separate races, but which are not and never have been separate from each other, there will be no more racial hatreds and fears among us. Thus we become wiser and more experienced thru natural growth as well as more complete and whole as a growing species, more fit to survive.

So let there be no more talk of racial or ethnic minorities, because in fact there are none. Rather, there are various members of the majority, a majority of 100%, peopled by all the Human Browns of this Earth. When we divide ourselves into different minority groups, each with its own priorities which often seem to be in conflict with all other priorities, what else can we expect to find within Human affairs but continuous and pointless family squabbles? It is simply not possible to satisfy the narrow demands of these countless minority groups without losing forever all hope of species union. For *Homo sapiens* to flourish as a gathered Family we must know that whether this or that person was born on this or that continent, or is of a lighter or darker Human Brown skin coloration, or was raised with one religious persuasion or another, is a trivial matter and has no significance whatsoever except for the particular individual involved.

When you hear speeches urging, for instance, a black separatist movement or boasting of Aryan white supremacy, then you should be aware that this is nothing but immature mob-talk and a real bore, as well as an active threat to the health of the Human family. In the first place you have named your colors wrongly, as there are no black or white people on this planet. If you do not even know the true color of your own Human Brown skin, then how much else of what you say on this subject can be trusted?

Also, as this not overly large planet is already crowded and overpopulated, just where do we intend for any separations within the race to take place? Because modern communication and transportation systems cause Earth to be a global village, how long do we think that any such separation could be maintained? Who needs the extra conflict and rivalry that would certainly result from even the attempt to bring about any such large separatist movements within the far larger species?

You need to grow up and mature, *Homo sapiens*, for the time has come when you have grown beyond your Human childhood. Allow yourselves to become aware of each other and of your larger family. Stop tormenting each other, stop persecuting yourselves because of racial variations within the species, variations which are shared by each one of you and which are so minor and insignificant that, in the mind of the Maker of the stars, they are non-existent.

As for the idea that any single group of Humans is somehow superior to everyone else, that is another bit of philosophical fluff that needs to be blown away by a living breath of healthy wind, out of sight and out of mind, a pile of Human crap that needs to be flushed down the nearest toilet. Thru out Human history such boasting brags of superiority have come from just about every continent, nation and city-state on Earth at one time or another, and those claims have always proved to be false. The mere making of such a boast is, by itself, a confession both of weakness and of fear; for truth proclaims itself and has no need to boast.

With everyone subject to the same Human frailties, with everyone needing the same food, water, and air in order to survive, with everyone clothed in the same Human Brown flesh and with all hearts pumping the same Human blood, and with everyone endowed with similar intellectual and spiritual capacity, give or take a few points here and there as the individual case might be, and with everyone filled with the same general potential for both vice and virtue, and with all of our bowels filled with the same basic fecal matter, then just how consistently could any widespread pattern of superiority and inferiority be upheld? Given the same educational opportunities, the differences between each of you are not nearly so great as all of you imagine. In fact, when seen from a distance, you each appear to exist within the same general parameters, as does everyone else.

We should read these words and, each one of us, imprint them deep inside our soul and pass this knowledge of ourselves onto our children. These racist fears, which have helped bring about the decline and fall of every major civilization that has yet arisen upon Earth, shall henceforth be ceased. Having landed and walked upon Luna, we are not children anymore. And while *Homo sapiens* are far from being an adult species, yet adult maturity is the eventual goal of our current puberty and adolescent growth. We are a family, and we must never, never, never forget that basic fact of life.

Love, intermarriage and childbirth among all the various peoples of the species, removing and forgetting all previous distinctions between them, shall be encouraged to flourish. A unity of thought and action within *Homo sapiens* is necessary at this time so that the natural growth of Humankind towards a fuller blooming may continue onward, much like the emergence of the fully revealed rose from the tightly packed bud, and like the butterfly awakening and coming forth from its caterpillar cocoon.

Tho to homogenize *Homo sapiens* is a needful step to take along the path of Human development, and must surely remove a mighty thorn from the side of Human civilization, yet I can see anger and great wrath as well as doubt among the peoples before true understanding cometh. But I must say again, *Homo sapiens*, that a species which is fractured and splintered within itself cannot survive among the stars. It is towards those stars that our new horizon now extends, to summon us forth in a forward march of the Human mind. We are biologically united, and this blood union is greater by far than any political, religious or ethnic separations within the gathered family might seem to be. Those differences are minor and have changed thru the centuries as do the seasons of the year, and yet the species abides. It is now, as we stand naked before the unknown void of the outer spaces, that we must come to know ourselves more thoroughly. So it must be a small matter as to which continent or nation was the original home of someone's ancestry, because those continents and nations are themselves but smaller parts of the larger planet.

Nor is there any need to worry ourselves overmuch concerning former days of slavery and of slave ownership. *There is not one single person now alive whose ancestors have not been, at one time or another, both enslaved as well as the enslavers of others.* Every one of us has been, as the centuries have rolled always onward like ocean waves rolling towards the beaches, both sinners and sinned against where any conditions of slavery and slave ownership have existed. Sufficient unto the day is the evil thereof, and as these words are written so let them be done and fully realized. As the past is gone in fact so let those past days be gone in fancy as well, so that the dead may bury the dead while Creation, for the living, goes ever onward.

The tendency to produce slavery is a terrible lure towards corrupt power, and does great damage to everyone involved. *The children of America must have learned this much, at least, during the Great War Between the States: That the practice of slavery is to be avoided, so as to avoid the inevitable Day of Atonement and national pain. The French aristocrats during the latter days of the 18th century, like the czarist Russians during the Bolshevik Revolution and like the Nazi supporters of war-torn Germany had the same knowledge enforced upon them: That slavery, whether for political, economic or religious reasons may not be allowed to flourish and fester, because the conclusion of such a cycle is always so dreadful to behold and endure. To avoid the bad ending of a bad meal, simply do not sit down at that particular table in the first place.* Learn to take your meals elsewhere and in better ways, *Homo sapiens*; and when you shall one day go out among the stars you must avoid the practice of slavery all together, as it is always best to avoid the very beginnings of evil.

Whenever Human slavery has been permitted to enter into daily business, then doom and social catastrophe have always followed soon thereafter. If we cannot learn that much, at least, then why bother to write or to read any books of Human history? What is the point of moving forward at all, if we cannot learn to avoid stubbing the same toes on the same hard rocks, again and again and again and again? If we wish to grow up and mature as a species, then let us learn how to learn from the events of past experience. Why should we believe ourselves to be thinking animals in the first place, unless we make some conscious effort to learn from the painful and hard-won lessons of previous days?

So we must now see that a great revolution lies before us. A revolution of thought is here, very much unlike any of the political revolutions that have occurred from time to time during the last few thousands of years. Here the great battlefield must be in the realm of the Human mind rather than in the streets, with outdated beliefs giving way and naturally changing into newer thoughts of fresh awareness.

No stacks of dead bodies need be piled high and then buried in mass graves in order for this revolution to succeed. No one need go to the wall and die before a firing squad, nor is it necessary that anyone be hanged by the neck until dead or be slid beneath the guillotine blade, nor do we need any streets to run with the blood of revolution's victims. All that is needed here is that you, *Homo sapiens*, sapient beings as you seem to be, awaken to this knowledge of who and what you are. Just as a person can remove and discard clothing which has become tattered and torn, so also can that same man or woman abandon beliefs which no longer answer the needs of a changed situation.

We are a species made of a few billions of diverse beings, none of whom is exactly like all the others, and each one of whom is deserving of some respect, at least, merely for the sake of the common Humanity which everyone shares with everyone else. It is to bring us together more closely that this great intermingling of all peoples of the species with each other is being done, to unite *Homo sapiens* in both theory and in fact also. In this way those racial prejudices, which die so hard, must soon pass away and be left behind as the species matures. This coming revolution, which has already begun, is one born from the needs of the changing biology of

Humankind and has been caused by the movement of Human history from one cycle of growth into the next highest level.

Law and Order

In <u>The Second Coming</u> the poet, thinking about the collapse and down falling of civilization, wrote thus:

Turning and turning in the widening gyre
The falcon cannot hear the falconer;
Things fall apart; the centre cannot hold;
Mere anarchy is loosed upon the world.
The blood-dimmed tide is loosed, and everywhere
The ceremony of innocence is drowned;
The best lack all conviction, while the worst
Are full of passionate intensity.
(William Butler Yates, 1865-1939)

Words more apt than these were never writ nor even thought before. In fact, these warnings are being fulfilled even now, with an exact certainty that is dreadful to behold and fearsome in its implications of great troubles soon to come. Some remedy must be found, else the Iceman cometh for us all.

As for things falling apart, just let us look at ourselves so as to see what we can see. Criminal deeds are being done everywhere and routinely, millions of times everyday upon this planet, on this small world of our birth, by ourselves and against each other, and with no considerations whatsoever as to the pain we cause each other by these rash actions upon ourselves. As individual members of the gathered family many of us have been guilty of serious misbehaviors at this time, the very bad type of wanton misbehaviors which seem to beg for the punishment of ill omens, for terrible prophecies to be fulfilled, and all toward an utter desolation for everyone concerned.

Drug addiction and public drunkenness are all over the place, as close to us as Human skin is. Acts of insanity and rabid viciousness are now a dime a dozen. Under the stresses of overpopulation and helped along by the toxic influence of the pollution poisons in Earth's atmosphere, we are even aborting our own babies and flushing them straight down the nearest toilet with no more apparent concern than if they were just so many carcasses of dead chickens, hogs and beef cattle usually found in any countryside slaughterhouse.

When we see our own babies being slain by voluntary or enforced abortion, and with such a rampant frequency as we have seen nowadays then we can know that bad times, insane times, the very worst of times, the times when normal sleeping brings no true refreshment to mind or body, have indeed come.

Of course all things are falling apart, because an entire age of the Human life cycle is itself falling apart. While we are now in the process of maturing beyond the age of Human childhood, we have only barely begun to greet our Human adolescence. During such transition times as these, it is the very uncertainty of it all that brings the threat. Thus while these are most surely times of great hope, these are also times of great danger for Humankind as well. For this reason, lest all be lost or damaged more severely, some steps must be taken so that too much does not fall apart too quickly or so totally as to then be beyond all hope of repair.

For instance, we are experiencing a complete and total breakdown of all normal law and order. We see an abundance of criminal deeds, which has excited wild alarm from within the whole of the Human community and is the feverish subject of so much public news and current gossip. This condition has caused many of us to be afraid of life itself, and so must now be addressed. The core of this plague of lawlessness lies in the widespread use of, and the arrogant smuggling of, illegal narcotic drugs. I am speaking here specifically of heroin, the methamphetamine speed drugs, and of cocaine derivatives. The smuggling of these drugs constitutes treason against the Human race and brings death by slow murder to the addict victims, and must therefore be punished by the strictest of hard laws.

We have heard it said that the war against illegal drugs has already been lost. Let us now believe instead that this war has not been lost but that we have not yet begun to fight. The time to begin is overdue, but late is better than never, and this is a case where a strong action in any direction is better than no actions whatsoever. This is a time when the fabled push has come to shove, so let us start shoving.

This is indeed a war, a war for law and order as opposed to moral chaos, a war of right against wrong, a war of Human freedom against the slavery and living death brought about by the massive narcotic addictions now being suffered thru out the whole of Human society.

It must be stopped, stopped here and now, before too much of this mere anarchy is further loosed upon the world. Desperate times require desperate measures. Therefore let there be a temporary suspension of civil liberties, a temporary suspension of the writ of *habeas corpus* in every nation now affected by this scourge. Six months should be time enough to do the job.

There was one time in particular, I remember, when I had an appointment to visit the dentist. I was only 7 or 8 yrs. old then, and I was eager to delay or even avoid altogether this visit. I suggested to my father that we not go there today, that if we waited for a few weeks then the afflicted tooth might heal itself. "Dental problems never get better," my father said, "they only get worse. You have to do it today."

In America, the influence of these narcotic drugs has provoked such a gluttony of criminal insanity that the rest of the world feels only horror and dismay to see such a sight. Nobody wishes for America to fall from greatness at this time, lest such a giant crash do great damage to us all. Yet such a fall remains a very real threat indeed, for so long as the American people continue to make no firm stand against this muddied river of corruption and moral decay. Moreover, America, it is just not in your national character or in the fiber of your American heart of hearts that you should roll over and play dead before this onslaught of crime. In times of war, wartime actions are needed, drastic tho such actions might seem to be, if the body politic hopes to endure and triumph thru this crisis of the Human spirit.

The smuggling of illegal narcotics represents the very worst aspects of Human greed.

This exploitation of Human weakness for the sake of mere gold and other filthy lucre is, in fact, a gross treason against Human survival by renegades and traitors from within the Human family. A successful campaign against this worst of all crimes must surely serve to restore a healthy respect for Human law and order all across the board and thru out the all to busy world of criminal activities.

"For the wages of sin is death," as was noted by Paul of Tarsus in his Epistle to the Romans, and death it shall be. Those wages must be remembered and exacted with full legal force, and with an active desire to remove and annihilate the treason being done here. Read and then read again Chapters 21 and 22 of *The Odyssey* by Homer, O ye children of *Homo sapiens*, and then you will know quite clearly what you must now do. The thoughts both of vengeance and of divine justice are hereby invoked, and for the purposes of cleaning a great House from the effects of gross and vulgar sin.

Many nations are now troubled by this frenzied and exhaustive ordeal of drug abuse from within the body of their peoples. America, a current focal point for much of the world's attention, would do well to show us all how best to act against this species emergency. America, as the leading user of these narcotics, must now help us all to vomit them from the Human body, and therefore from the Human soul as well.

The U. S. Constitution allows for two occasions of national emergency wherein martial law may be declared and the writ of habeas corpus be briefly *set aside*. * If the federal government is confronted by either a foreign

---

*Please see U.S. Constitution: Article 1, Section 9, Paragraph 2

invasion or by a civil rebellion then martial law may legally be invoked, so that the emergency might not prove fatal to the state. Abraham Lincoln suspended the writ of *habeas corpus* during the War Between the States while Jefferson Davis either did not or could not enforce any action which went so directly contrary to the Confederate doctrine of States' Rights as this would have been, and history tells us which side won.

There are occasions, such as in these present circumstances, when treason and sedition must be suppressed. *A concentration of the national will, a gathering together of national forces with a single goal in mind, and freed from the distraction caused by the babble and chatter of confused, uninformed voices is essential at this time and in this situation.*

Here, there is both a foreign invasion from outside sources as well as a civil rebellion against state and federal laws. There is therefore legal justification and the historical precedent also, as well as a moral need to do so, for the declaration of temporary martial law so as to maintain order during a time of national crisis. Moreover there is a sickness among the people, a general malaise caused by the boredom of constant sinning and being sinned against, and that sickness must be cured.

You cannot survive as a nation, America, against this onslaught of threats both foreign and domestic, and which strike so deeply at your most basic national morality. Is life even worth living, when your cities have degenerated into savage jungles of crazed and drug-inspired warfare? Now look ye here, America, and consider well: When so many of your sons and daughters as well as your friends and neighbors are living numbed, half-dead lives in a zombie existence; when there is no general respect for law and order nor for public and personal morality either; and when you see the spilling in the streets of our American heart's blood and the loss of national integrity also; then is that any kind of a good life to be lived in this, the land of the free and the home of the brave?

Iksander, ruling in ancient days, taught us that when a complex and tangled knot is too convoluted to be easily untied, but which must be untied nevertheless for the sake of survival both personal and political, then you must cut and slash that knotted rope with firm dispatch and a sharp sword, and with not so much debate involved. Stop talking so much, you sons and daughters of America, and act! Hack this Gordian knot with the sharpest sword you can find and go on from there.

Declare a limited time of martial law, aimed specifically at the arrest and incarceration of these bastard drug barons who have been hiding behind the shield of normal democratic freedoms and legal procedures. Give a top priority mission to all police and law enforcement personnel that the narcotic drug traffic in America is to be crushed, crushed as the head of a venomous snake in the grass must be crushed, for the sake of Human health. The apprehended criminals are to be prosecuted in the courts under the weight of heavy laws. Those found guilty of murder and treason against the species shall be put to death. Sooner or later the killer shall be killed, the traitor betrayed into death and ruin.

In further pursuit of the American battle campaign against the heavy traffic in illegal narcotics, find and appoint a man who strongly resembles in word and in deed the late American war leader, General George S. Patton, to command the U. S. Coast Guard. Grant him full and total authority in dealing with this problem. His marching orders, to end all drug smuggling into America by sea and air, are simple and clear.

These drug bosses and their gangs have learned to love the taste of honey and are well armed, and there is no doubt that their briberies and threats of blackmail have reached into high places by now. Therefore, there may well be the need to send in the U. S. Marines, and to summon the U. S. Army, Navy, and Air Force besides. If other nations require military aid and military personnel in order to subdue these destroyers of Human civilization, America, then you must provide such help at once.

This is very much in your own best domestic interests, and must also help to stabilize the entire Western world as well. From Russia, Japan, the nations of western Europe, to both North and South America, and in Australia also, this cancer of narcotic drug traffic must be removed, by military and political surgery if necessary, from the spirit and the body of Humankind.

As for those among us who fear the temporary loss of civil liberties, and who fear the imposition of a permanent dictatorship, I say that it were better to suffer such risks rather than to allow further success to these criminal rogues, and for our greater loss and national death. Where are the freedom and the joy of living if people cannot walk the streets by day or night without the threats of robbery, assault and murder running close behind them? Where's the pleasure and the normal fun of life, if we cannot simply live and be happy? How can any worthwhile Human activities be accomplished or even begun, when so many members of the general population are leading drunken or drug-addicted lives, and when so many others from among the species entire are helping them to do so? Clearly some decisive action is required here, America. Those steps which you have already taken, to hire more police officers, legislate more laws and build bigger prisons, have not been effective so far and never will be. Such cosmetic cures, easy, convenient and expedient as they most surely are, will not end this disease so long as the source of the infection remains intact.

Various people, for their own criminal, political or philosophical reasons are pumping these narcotics into your national bloodstream. Thus your national spirit is under attack, America. This will continue until that flow of noxious medicine has been ended and the freedom of the streets, the freedom and joy of ordinary living, is regained and made good again.

America! Your own democratic procedures are being used against you by criminals to make dumb stooges of you all, and to turn your judicial system into a farce and a mockery of legal justice which is ridiculed by everyone and which no one feels compelled to obey. When you impose a temporary application of martial law so as to halt all traffic in narcotic drug smuggling you will, with one swift stroke of the sharp sword untie a very tangled knot, and restore your strength of purpose into the most fundamental ideals of law, domestic order, and the spiritual health of American civilization. *It is precisely during such times as these, when hurricane winds are raging in fullest fury across the ocean waves, that the ship's crew must batten down the hatches, tie down and secure all loose cargo and maintain their strictest maritime discipline, or else the ship of state might sink and the body politic be drowned in spilled blood.*

Fear and Knowledge

But there is a deeper question to be answered here, and that is this: Why do so many of our peoples continue to seek the vain and stupid pleasures of these narcotic drug addictions? The use of these drugs is bad for the Human soul, as everyone knows full well. So why do we continue to use them and to love them so much, and to allow the use of these narcotic pleasure drugs to spread wider and cut more deeply into the greater body of the gathered Family?

You see all around you that these drug addicts soon lose both their personal beauty as well as the health of their bodies. You see the numbing of their minds, so that life seems dead to them. You see that they lose all joy of living and that their pleasures take on a frantic quality of desperation which brings them no refreshment, no surcease of pain, but only spiritual exhaustion and a desolation of the Human soul.

Therein resides the question: Why do so many of us find these temptations to be so tempting? When we see dogs licking up vomit in the streets, why do we then rush to do the same? Is it absolutely necessary, or even desirable, that we should degrade ourselves and each other so eagerly and with such apparent delight? How is it that the taste of vomit from the gutter seems to be so delicious to us? What is the problem here? What are we doing to ourselves, and why?

Thru out Human history, whenever you see entire communities of Humankind being so thoroughly affected by widespread public drunkenness and drug addiction as we see today, *Homo sapiens*, you may take that as a certain sign that there is a great and terrible fear upon the people. Here, the effect of the fear has been so great because the cause of the fear is likewise great.

By taking our first steps upon Luna we have entered into a vast and unknown territory. We know and feel within ourselves that *Homo sapiens* is close to, or even in excess of, the limits of our physical growth on this planet. But we do not yet know where to go from here or what to do next and, being sensible creatures, we are naturally afraid. It is this subconscious fear of the unknown and nighttime dark that has sent out ripples of confusion thru out the Human world and has caused all Human affairs to seem so troubled, so doubtful.

This is why, as the poet wrote,

> "Things fall apart; the centre cannot hold;
> mere anarchy is loosed upon the world.
> The blood-dimmed tide is loosed,
> and everywhere the ceremony of innocence is drowned;
> the best lack all conviction,
> while the worst are full of passionate intensity."

These problems, then, must come and can only be coming from fear and from fear alone. It is during such times, when the purpose and the home destination of the voyage is uncertain that the lotus-eaters among us, the chronic drunkards and the narcotic drug addicts among us, feel most strongly the heavy weight of their own spiritual panic and lack of faith. Seeking and embracing the temptations of easy living, they begin to ruin themselves and bring great disruptions to all of Human society.

Yet I say to you now, *Homo sapiens*: Do not take counsel from your fears. Because in truth, this is yet another occasion when you have nothing to fear but fear itself. The Maker of all things has also made you, *Homo sapiens*. Sons and daughters of Creation, read this and learn well! We have not been made to walk upon this white stone named Luna merely because the time for doom and Human extinction has come. But rather you must now know that this has been but your first step taken into a new Heaven and a new Earth, the dawning of a fresh new day whose arrival has been foretold since the very beginning of the ages.

Therefore, boys and girls, these many crimes in the streets and in your homes do not become you. We are a better peoples than such a feverish rash of criminal deeds would indicate, and we are smart enough to know that this is true. The cleansing of Earth from the effects of industrial pollution requires a global effort of hard work from every person now alive. This hard work towards a definite goal is our salvation: Earth is to be cleaned, the moons and planets of this solar system are to be colonized, and the galaxy explored. And if worldwide boredom has been any part of the problem, then these types of labors must be our response.

We cannot escape our destiny by hiding behind booze and drugs, my young children of Humankind. By attacking each other we are wasting the natural energies of outward expansion in a foolish attempt to avoid moving into a future which has seemed doubtful to us up until now. That doubt, that lack of faith, is the real reason behind this global breakdown of law and order. Knowing this, knowing the cause of the fear, we must now accept the responsibilities inherent in our growth towards species adulthood. Rather than confronting the larger problems of species survival we are turning our aggressive attacks against each other, and the situation is just as simple as that.

Even tho we feel the need to grow we have not yet realized the direction of the growing. It is as if an unhatched eagle, not yet understanding the process of hatching and with no knowledge of the blue skies and high clouds and gusty headwinds soon to be flown, were to peck savagely at its own breast instead of against the inside of its eggshell enclosure. For that is exactly what we are doing right now, *Homo sapiens*. We are fighting amongst ourselves, in a frightened avoidance of any outward growth and expansion from this egg of Earth.

We need to grow up and act our age. Grow up, I say again. For the love of Creation, and as we are the children of Creation, let us wake up and grow up and look to see the stars that shine in the dark void around us, as we now seek to move ourselves closer towards their far and distant fire.

Further Law and Order

The basic laws are easy to understand. No society can have any stability where its members feel free to commit murder upon each other. Therefore, the deliberate murder with malicious intent by any Human of another shall be cause for the penalty of death.

Treason against the species, crimes against Humanity for reasons of political power, or for financial gain, must also be seen as just cause for the penalty of death. The attempt to spread the use of narcotic pleasure drugs among the children of the Human family must fall under this law, and the true payment for such a crime of treason shall be death for the offender.

There has been much debate during recent years concerning the need for, and the efficacy of, the use of the death penalty as a punishment for crimes committed, such as when murder or treason is done. Some people say that because criminals always hope and believe that they will not be apprehended anyway, then that means that the threat of a death penalty will have no effect upon their plans and therefore serves as no deterrent. Also, we have heard that the use of the death penalty involves a cruel and unusual punishment, and so should not be done for that reason. Also you have heard that Human society, by executing convicted criminals has itself become a murderer, and so we must attempt to rise above the need for bloodlust and petty revenge for the sake of the ideals of Human purity and for the respect due to Human life. Further, because so many murders are done in a moment of high passion in which no thought of right or wrong or of any punishment to come might be considered, then the death penalty might be avoided in those cases as well.

And what happens when an innocent person is convicted and then executed for a crime which he or she did not commit?

Except for this last question, which has no satisfactory answer at this time but that blood must sometimes be the price of Admiralty, these arguments miss the basic idea. That idea is this: That Human civilization must continue to grow or else all Human society shall pass away totally, to be forgot and with no purpose served, no Human truth to be found and lived, no light without ending ever to be seen and known, and with no Human potential to be filled and enriched by the experience of living.

As for those people for whom the fear of death serves as no deterrent for their murders or treasons against Humankind, they must be slain and removed from the species for the sake of species survival, if for no other reason. Those who are so stupid as to be undeterred from the act of murder by the active threat of legal execution to come in repayment for such murder, they shall be legally executed and the threat fulfilled, forthwith and with quickest speed.

As to the use of the death penalty being a cruel and unusual punishment, let us remember that the death penalty has been used against arrant citizens since recorded time began, and so there is nothing unusual about that. As for the cruelty involved, just consider the cruelty done to the victims of murderous behaviors and then relax in the knowledge that basic justice has occurred.

People who kill other people, even tho there might be insanity involved or precisely because of that insanity involved, must be removed from the species. The presence of insanity, by itself and with the Mc Naughten rule to be reconsidered, is no legal or moral defense for murder. People who are so crazed that they cannot live without killing other people shall be slain, like as when a surgeon removes the cancerous cells from a malignant tumor so that the patient might be cured of an illness. In this case the patient is *Homo sapiens*, the species entire, and we cannot allow ourselves to be stopped now simply because some of us have gone mad with fear during these days of growth and transition. These times are special times, times when intense passion has become the general rule of order. But even during normal days the wanton, brutal and ill-considered murder of Human beings by each other shall not be allowed.

If we wish that the death penalty be abolished, then there is a very easy solution to that question. If and when you, the Human children, wish that there were no more death penalties invoked then you, the Human children, must stop committing death penalty crimes, and the answer is just as simple as that. *Those who would preach against the use of the death penalty would do far better to preach against murder or treason, for that is how the question will finally be solved.*

For these people who cannot control their high passions even to the point of doing hasty murders, then let them also be legally executed or be further educated, just as children with temper tantrums are taught not to inflict their tantrums upon others. Animals with rabies must be slain or cured, for the safety of all the other creatures nearby, and so it must be likewise with ourselves.

A society whose members feel free to commit wanton brutalities upon each other cannot hope to find and establish any form of true civilization. There shall be law and order within Human society. There shall be law and order within Human society, or else there shall be no Human society whatsoever.

Also, there is a massive congestion of convicted criminals within the various prisons now in use. Within those crowded prisons an entire society has evolved, wherein convicted felons languish for years in enforced boredom and stagnation. With all normal comforts of life freely provided so that they can live lives of comparative ease and happy security, learning no lessons of right and wrong but having their individual lives wasted away, and with no advantage gained either for the individual prisoner or for Human society, this entire penal system is a complete waste of time and money and Human effort. In such an atmosphere of concentrated criminality all criminal behaviors are being positively reinforced on a daily basis within the prison population, just thru the normal conversation and social interaction between prisoners.

Thus the released prisoner has frequently become a much more destructive person than he or she had been before the prison confinement began. Moreover, all of this is being done with a great wastage of years and money, and with a loss of the potential growth for Human talent also.

Nothing good is being accomplished by the long prison confinements of convicted criminals. Let us find a means of punishment that can be done in a short time, in the certain knowledge that a Human being has the animal ability to learn from a bad experience. In former times there was flogging with the whip, so as to provide both chastisement and the need to learn for the offender. Nowadays, in some nations of the world strokes from a bamboo cane, and well laid on, are used to punish minor offenses.

In serious cases, where murder or treason has been done, then execute the offender and be done with it. Let justice be done, and then move on from there. Otherwise, this prison population is going to grow and grow and grow until, perhaps, the whole planet is covered by prisons. How many more prisons do we plan to build, anyway?

Whatever the case may be, we must punish the offender forthwith and cease enforcing these long prison terms which do no good for anyone involved and only make the problem worse. If society must punish and chastise, or educate the criminals, then do so quickly and cleanly. A few sharp strokes with a bamboo cane rather than two or three years spent in useless, idle boredom would better suit the needs of the day, and would reduce this overcrowded prison population by as much as 80%.

At least half the number of all lawyers, with their delaying tactics that often amount to no more than verbal and esoteric meanderings, should be disbarred and released from service so that they can seek some form of employment more conducive to the health and progress of Human society. Human affairs simply cannot move forward while our minds and feet are entangled by so many legal webs and snares as we have now built for ourselves. Close down at least half of all the law schools, because too many lawyers, as is the case with too many cooks, spoil the broth. Argument for the sake of mere argument followed by more legal arguments that seem to go on and on with no end in sight nor with any questions firmly answered might help the lawyers in their pursuit of wealth and political influence, but the process and its results have certainly impoverished everyone else.

Let us tear down and destroy some of these prisons, as they make waste of the countryside and of the Human spirit also. Set a standard whereby trials are conducted more quickly, and without so many legal gestures and other forms of legal movements, procedures and writs of this or that or of something else. Establish a system wherein the criminal is shown that criminal behavior is not productive, but is painful instead. Execute and remove those who cannot live within the species without brutalizing their neighbors. Whatever it is to do, you must act to remove the bloated congestion from within these prisons. Punish them quickly, and then let them get busy with the normal living of their lives. What else is the purpose of Human life but for the healthy Human living of it, with the health of the individual and of society both to be encouraged, after all?

Yet the entire legal system does no good at all unless we, each one of us, wish to produce and maintain a society that is wholesome and generally healthy for everyone. We are not meant, *Homo sapiens*, to be a species of murderers, thieves, and liars. We are meant to be, and must be as we grow towards the adult maturity of our kind, a species of gardeners and farmers, builders of true civilization, teachers and seekers of knowledge, givers of light and makers of fire.

There are rules to be followed, as the guideposts and signs set upon a path that winds its way thru a dark forest must be followed by any lone traveler. Similarly, as *Homo sapiens* grows and matures thru the ages those signs and guideposts are followed so that good food and shelter can be found, the full glory of Human growth achieved, all Truth to be realized and made known, and with a warm home of eternal light waiting at the end of the path.

The evolution of *Homo sapiens* has a goal and a direction in mind, and is to fulfill the will of Creation. Have we not always known that much, at least? Can we not see and understand that there must be a purpose behind the growth of Human civilization, or else why has such a potential for further growth occurred at all? If there were no possibility for a rose to fully bloom itself, or for a mighty oak tree to grow and to thrive, or for a butterfly to take wing and fly upon the wind, then why have a rosebud or an acorn to exist in the first place? Why should nature cause the butterfly caterpillar to live for any reason, if there were no possibility for further growth to come? There is growth being done here, and growth aplenty! There is growth being done both within and all around ourselves, as the species entire grows towards the full blooming of the Human flower. If a great oak tree can grow from a dropped acorn or if a butterfly can emerge from the caterpillar's cocoon, then just imagine what might be the higher goal of our own evolving condition.

The light of divine truth, which has always inspired the finest of Human thought and yet remains unseen and unseeable by Human sight, shall one day be revealed from the Human soul with a glory and a brilliance far brighter than the hottest of stars could ever know. When Human history has grown thru the full cycle of the Human life, when *Homo sapiens* is united again with the true source of all Creation then on that day we shall be as one with the Light, fully conscious and self-aware, knowing at long last who and what we are and always have been. Yes, and you shall know the truth when you see the truth, for you shall be the truth. Meanwhile, there must be order in Human society and so there must be some individual effort, at least, to obey those laws which define that social order. Instead of bemoaning the current fever of criminal behaviors, each of us needs to pay more attention to his or her individual actions and stop being those criminals. Who do we think has been doing all those murders and robberies, anyway? It is not the dogs and the cats that have been doing these crimes, and I can say that much right now, and in certain truth.

It is we, boys and girls, whose criminal deeds are now the cause of so much public discussion and have provoked such general fears among ourselves. What? Did we think that the birds and the fishes have somehow been the secret villains behind this massive crime wave, or that it has been the goats and the monkeys who have been doing these things?

If so, then think again. Let us think again, and think better this time. Look in a mirror and there is a very good chance that you will see, looking back at you, the face of someone who is far more personally involved in this global carnival of murder, robbery and brutal assault than the birds and the fishes ever were. Therefore, rather than building bigger prisons and hiring more police officers, we must grow up as a peoples and stop committing so many crimes against ourselves. How do you like that, boys and girls? How do you like that for a radical solution to the problem? Cease committing crimes against each other, you sons and daughters of Creation. What are we, anyway? Is this a moral species of Human beings, and endowed with a sense of creative intelligence, or are we just another pack of wild and savage dogs? Are we a species of potentially sapient beings? Or are we a pack of wild dogs who must attack and kill each other for reasons of food and sex, leaving the dead and bloodied bodies behind us and with no knowledge and sense of truth gained?

Too many people think that they can commit crimes and then escape the legal penalties because of their personal wealth, political influence, or clever wit. Frequently this might appear to be true, that crime pays and pays well. But do not be fooled. Those who appear to have avoided legal penalties must still meet their Maker on that day when they must pass into the next life. The Human soul is eternal, not so easily perished, as is this body of Earthly flesh and blood. You who disobey the laws of ancient days shall be judged then, a judgment from which there is no escape or avoidance. If in your soul, wherein you should be filled with light and be always seeking to know the light, instead from the knowledge of personal sin, then all of your everyday living shall be further darkened as your soul rots and withers away like a fruit that dies on the vine. Thru all eternity, no one ever gets away with anything, and all sins are repaid in full measure.

Let this be the law of Humankind and the basic code of Human behavior, to serve as the guide towards Human morality, and so be passed on from each generation unto the next:

You shall not commit murder;

You shall not commit theft;

You shall not speak lies;

You shall not commit adultery.

Yes, and you shall not be the enemy of your own kind, nor shall you be creatures of prey upon them nor they upon you, for we of *Homo sapiens* shall love each other and be a gathered Family. Above all else we must remember what was said by both Siddhartha and by Jesus, that "You shall do unto others as you would have done unto you." There is a law of mathematical certitude being spoken here: That exactly and to the precise degree that whatever one does to other people shall be likewise repaid precisely and even without any knowledge that the moment of repayment cometh, and yet that moment cometh nevertheless. For good or for bad, whatever is done shall be repaid in full, and your behavior towards your fellows must and shall be returned unto you with a fine exactness.

There is no need for any deep thought here, nor for any esoteric philosophies to be discussed concerning this most basic code of moral behavior and of Human existence: That whatever you would not have done unto yourself, do not do the same unto others. Rather, a sense of simple decency and of basic hospitality are all we need to remember, as well as the abiding faith that the Creator who has made us also loves us, each and every one. Where the laws of cause and effect rule, not merely by poetic faith but in reality as well, the laws of cause and effect must rule with full and constant Will. If you beat other people or stab them with a knife, or shoot them with a gun or steal from them, or tell lies to them, or enslave others, or otherwise deliberately harm other creatures merely for reasons of personal greed or for wealth and political power, or to satisfy the need for warped and neurotic pleasures, or to soothe your own guilty conscience by killing those who have rebuked you justly, then such transgression shall be repaid and made good. This full repayment always happens, and not only because the teachings of ancient days say so but also because the mathematical and inexorable progression of cause and effect, the certitude that action always causes precise and specific reaction to occur, says so as well.

Think Thought,
and Goeth Thou Forth

Well, boys and girls, this century of Human affairs has been a fairly busy time for the species entire, has it not? After several major wars and national revolutions, the political landscape of our home planet has been wholly remade. New theories of economics and of government have had their effects upon our thinking. Medical knowledge, scientific discovery and religious thought have all been moved forward, so that we now find ourselves to be living in a fresh world which we have made, and which we must now embrace and strive to further increase.

The harmful effects of industrial pollution must be cleaned away from the homeworld, and so we are faced with both the opportunity and the strong need for the building of an entirely new system of Human technology. The World Union of Earth has yet to be fully formed and inaugurated, but that day is coming soon. Also *Homo sapiens* has now walked upon Luna, so that the dawning of a new age is now as clear as the springtime budding in a green forest is clear to wild animals of the woodlands, clean and fresh before us, thus inviting our further and most eager perusal. Of all the events and occasions of this century, however, none has provided a more exact example of the species entire caught in a moment of its own biological growth, and caught in fullest action also, as has been seen in the emergence of what we have called the Women's Liberation movement.

We see that a time has come when the female of the species seems to be taking a wider interest in Human affairs. We see significant achievements being done by the female in all the arts and sciences, and in economic and political activities as well. We see that this movement is not limited to any one nation or region of the world nor is restricted to any specific political or religious school of thought. Moreover, this does not appear to be a phenomenon which will simply go away and be forgot, but will instead continue to flourish until all Human civilization is informed.

The information to be received is this: *That what we have known as Women's Liberation is caused by the biological growth of <u>Homo sapiens</u> from its infancy, childhood, then now into its puberty and adolescent stage of development; that our landing upon Luna signals the beginning of that adolescence; and that the Human female tends to feel the onset of puberty a little sooner than does the Human male.*

You are growing, *Homo sapiens*, as the history of Human life continues onwards towards species adulthood. Hence the Women's Liberation movement has come, and thence have all the books been written and the fine speeches been made on this subject. Thus have all the Human passions been stirred into near frenzy as the basic relationship between man and woman seems to have been shaken to the very core of the Human soul. This has never been a question of paid salaries and other economic considerations, nor of political freedoms, nor of greater or lesser intellect, nor even of moral goodness, but is instead a biological awakening in which each man and woman of the species has been but an unconscious agent up until now.

As is the case with all living things, *Homo sapiens*, we are always in constant growth. What we are experiencing in these days is a moment of growth climax wherein the basic biology of the species is awakening into the changes brought about by natural maturation, a movement into Human adolescence, and with the thoughts of *Homo sapiens* adult always in mind. We are becoming young adults, boys and girls. And it is this changing of the fundamental Human condition, the adolescent glandular secretions of it all, which has caused such a shake-up within the species to occur. The full effects of these adolescent glandular secretions upon our thinking must be fully addressed and answered within the *spiritus mundi* and body politic of the gathered Family.

1.

Overpopulation tensions have produced more anxieties within the Human mind, as has the fear of a nuclear war that would be too large for this small world to endure. Also, the polluting of Earth's food, water and air supplies must have damaged or somehow hindered Human thought processes by now, and must have also damaged our Human reproductive abilities as well. Ergo, we can surely understand that the doubt, the global confusion and primal fear as to the future of Humankind are not wholly without due cause.

When we realize that there is a reason and a purpose behind the apparently endless madness of these times, and that there is a direction of growth to be found even in the very midst of this global confusion, then many of our worst anxieties and questions will answer themselves and simply vanish away. For instance, observe the growing popularity of male and female homosexuality. Of course, members of the same sex have been engaging in sexplay with each other since before the first pyramids were built. But why has homosex come to be so prolific and so apparently virtuous at this particular moment of Human history, and during this time of millennial turning?

The Human race, comprising billions of living beings, is itself alive and sentient, and is aware of its surroundings. Thus there is a basic knowledge from within the *spiritus mundi*, heard and known within the vast murmurations of all the collected and individual peoples of the race, that this planet is overpopulated by Humankind. The spreading acceptance of homosexuality, a sexual behavior that is completely non-reproductive of offspring, must represent a subconscious effort by the species entire to limit its size and rate of growth. Let me state this again: ***The sudden and massive spread of homosexuality, a sexual behavior which is completely non-reproductive of offspring, must represent a subconscious effort by the species entire to limit its size and rate of growth.***

Those of us who have argued the good or the bad of homosex, its virtue or the total lack thereof, and often with violence and further anger as the only result of such debate have all been the unknowing pawns of biological forces which, up until now, have been beyond our present understanding. Most of the sexual tensions we are experiencing nowadays, both as a species or as individuals of the species, are those same tensions which are always felt when childhood begins to grow into adolescence. This is just a part of growing up, and it happens to all maturing youngsters.

In the larger world of natural order, there is nothing new in this. Rabbit does who become pregnant in an overcrowded warren, for instance, will absorb the unborn embryos back into their bodies. Goldfish in a goldfish bowl will grow to be only of a small size; whereas those same goldfish, when born into a larger body of water will grow to be likewise larger. Various species of insects and other animals, such as locusts, Army or Driver ants, and lemmings will launch destructive and even suicidal rampages in order to escape conditions of overcrowding.

Thus we must understand that there is no question here of moral depravity or of any conscious desire to do evil and be wicked. Rather we see a biological imperative being expressed in basic terms of everyday living: That the species will either act in such ways as to limit its size according to the amount of food and territory available, or else we will find more territory in which to grow and flourish. Other and less fortunate methods of limiting our population include nuclear war and global plague.

Whereas, making this planet more healthy by cleansing away our industrial polluting of its natural resources, finding more food and improving food distribution within the species, as well as colonizing the various planets and moons of this solar system while also looking outwards toward the further galaxy beyond, must surely relieve those self-same stresses caused by planetary overpopulation. As this species moves to establish itself into wider territories and finds room for further growth, then both the need and the desire for homosex will be naturally reduced into more normal levels of usage.

2.

Yet in these times of desperation and fear, when the very future of the Human race is itself uncertain and in serious doubt there have been, in fact, basic questions asked concerning Human morality and sexual awareness. We seem to be obsessed with our own genital passions, obsessed with our own sexual appetites, obsessed to the point of mania with our own and with each other's sexual proclivities, so obsessed with desires of the flesh that sexual lovemaking between man and woman becomes more like an act of masturbation rather than of procreation and of life renewing itself. This is yet another aspect of Human adolescence seeking to find itself, and is a normal part of growing up that happens to all maturing youngsters.

But there is a fuller story to be told now, straight and true, concerning the origin of the Human life and of sexual desire. In the beginning of the Human life man and woman, now separate from each other, were a whole being. Biologically complete and capable of self-reproduction, our primal Human beast with two backs was at rest in the dormant quietude of hermaphrodite perfection. Just so was Creation done within the warm ocean womb of Mother Earth. Earth conceived the Human child, as Mother was made pregnant by the divine light and seed of God as the Father of all Creation, with male and female fully joined together into one being.

So that growth could continue towards a fuller fruition this primal jelly was split into its male and female parts. Man and Woman are the children of those two parts, as the basic instincts of life to create and renew itself having been given flesh and made real.

There is the true story of Adam and Eve now told unto thee; and how else could the will of Creation have been made manifest, if not in such a way? There is and there must be a biological explanation for the origin of life which fulfills, in earlier and deeper truth, the various allegories of religious fable which have been so thoroughly accepted by us up until now. It has been the constant rubbing of man and woman against each other, and the hot friction produced when man and woman rub against each other, always opposing yet always seeking completion with each other that causes the further generation of *Homo sapiens* to occur.

The whole history of mating and of marriage, of courtship and of the search for true love eternal, of argument and sexual rivalry, of the birth of children and the spread of family ties, have all been caused by the need of that primordial Human protoplasm to reunite with itself. The desire of man and woman for each other is therefore dominant above all else and paramount. The basic sexual drive of *Homo sapiens* is therefore heterosexual, as the essential growth of man and woman is ultimately towards each other and to be married into one flesh again.

Anyone who looks at the physical structure of the Human body can see, clearly enough, that man and woman are formed as two halves of the same whole puzzle. From one origin and source have you come, ye children of *Homo sapiens*; and it is the rejoining of yourself, conscious and fully aware, that you are finally growing towards. Yet that time of true marriage cometh not until the age of Human adolescence matures and you emerge, more fully grown, as *Homo sapiens* adult.

3.

By the way, what is the meaning behind all these abortions being done nowadays? For what reason has *Homo sapiens* begun to conspire within itself and slay, unborn and unloved, so many Human babies?

And I care nothing whatsoever for these legal justifications of abortion, neither for any decisions made by judges nor for legislative acts of Congress, and not for any political theories and esoteric discussions concerning personal freedoms. Because, the true fact of the matter is this: *Homo sapiens* as a young species is afraid to grow up, is afraid of the dark, and so is most fearful of going forward from the homeworld into the darkness beyond Luna.

Why else would we be so eager to abort the children who must follow in our footsteps, if this were not the case? Why else, if we did not fear the unknown path those footsteps must soon travel? We have wished to flee the terrors of a future we have not yet comprehended, and so we are aborting our own children with this wild abandonment of all true since of our own further Creation. We are making war upon the next generation of Humankind because we fear for our own survival, and we seek to abort our babies so as to justify those fears and make them come true. The proliferation of Human abortion represents, above all else, the complete loss of hope for the future growth of *Homo sapiens*. This is a sin, a sin bred and born from despair, and comes from our own lack of any true vision as to both the immediate future of our kind and for the fuller destiny of Human growth.

Tho I am not a physician and have no more than a common knowledge of medicine, I nevertheless know enough to recognize an acute symptom when I see one, even if I might not know what specific illness or disease is indicated.

Thus when I see that millions of Human babies are being aborted every year by man and woman, that the urgent urge of life to live is itself being deliberately frustrated even at the very moment of quickening, and for legal justifications which seem to be false, contrived and less than fully convincing, then I know that something, something, something is wrong and in error on the most fundamental level of Human biology and in Human morality as well.

Everyone knows that Earth is overly populated by Humankind. But do we seriously believe that by aborting so many millions of our babies that we will provide any relief at all for this tightly packed and crowded condition? In some nations we hear about shortages of food. Well then, we must grow more food, we must find more food, or we must make our own food, and then distribute such food more efficiently than we have done up until now.

Desert wastelands can be irrigated so as to make room for farms and further agriculture. We can build undersea farms, reaping our harvest from the ocean floor. When we turn the focus of our attention away from the building of military weapons and weapon delivery systems and more towards the survival of Humankind, then we will be able to find the time and the resources necessary to address the threat of global starvation. *Homo sapiens* cannot, merely because these are times of urgent peril, simply abort our own babies so as to shrink backwards from further growth. In fact, the biological growth of our peoples and the greater expansion of species territory is precisely what is needed here. Because, in this particular moment of our history there is the true desire to grow outwards from this home planet of Human genesis, and that desire shall be fulfilled unto the point of a natural imperative of expansion.

This might not always be so. As when an oak tree eventually achieves its mature potential for height and depth and width then just so will we, *Homo sapiens*, eventually realize our own full potential as to size and numbers. But that time is not yet here. At present, when compared to a fully grown oak tree we are still very young, a sapling species in growth. To fully clean our homeworld, make finer systems of technology for ourselves, and to reach outwards also in seeking new territories on which to expand and flourish, is the best and only way to ease this current congestion of overpopulation now pressing inwards upon the Human family.

Also we have heard that because a child goes thru gestation inside the mother's womb, then she should have freedom of choice between abortion and giving birth. However, any man or woman who does not wish to have birth occur can avoid the whole question by avoiding promiscuous and irresponsible sexual lovemaking in the first place. What is this, that we should wish to enjoy the many pleasures of life but do none of the work of life, the work with which the living of life is most concerned? Is life just a big juicy fruit pie for us, that we should eat slice after delicious slice of the pie but then give no thought or care as to the making and the baking of the pie? Do we think that life is just a bed of roses, with no thorns involved?

This idea of free will which many of us seem to find so delightful, an idea of free choice which many of us have expressed by choosing to abort our own babies rather than to give birth to them must provoke this question: If the idea of making a free choice is important to us as a means of living, then why do we choose to make death rather than to give life?

Let us ask ourselves why, why, why have so many pregnancies resulted in abortion rather than in birth? Since when in all of Human history has the coming together of romance and love between man and woman been used as the means whereby Human babies are aborted from within the womb, and then flushed down the nearest toilet like so much Human waste? Is the seed of man, then, of no value whatsoever, nor are his desires of procreation? Is woman's womb now to be no more than a Nazi death-camp in waiting? Are all thoughts of Human romance, love and purest hope now to be turned into just another garbage dump of discarded junk? Is there to be nothing but the discarded refuse of Human filth, with no hope of the purest Human fire ever to be revealed?

How many abortions must we do, *Homo sapiens*, before we sicken of them and from the very idea of them? How many of our own babies must we devour before we grow sick from the taste of them?

When will we realize that making this atmosphere of abortion is wrong, biologically and morally wrong for a living species to do to itself, and has poisoned our personal relationships in ways we have not yet understood?

With the urge of life to be lived that has always struggled and thrived within the Human soul, is abortion the very best example of life being lived and freely expressed that we can offer in fulfillment of our own Creation?

Have we not yet learned that in this universe where the law of cause and effect always rules, where every action begets an equal reaction and when that reaction itself triggers further reaction, and so forth *ad infinitum*, that we cannot safely abort our own babies without losing the basic integrity that holds together the Human marriage, and without the loss of true passion as well? We might as well try to believe that we can drop a large handful of dirt into a bowl of clean water while hoping that no dirty water will then be made.

Do we really believe, in our Human heart of hearts, that we can safely engage in such greedy behaviors with no thought of the spiritual damage that we might be doing to ourselves and to each other as a result? If so, then let us take a clear, close look at ourselves and at the faces of the people around us, and think again.

Just as dry dirt will and must make mud when it is dropped into a bowl of clean water, just so will the influence of abortion make the guilt, the suppressed anger and neurotic boredom, the fear and the grief that we see on the faces of people we meet everyday. When abortion is introduced into Human biology as a moral goodness, mud must result.

For instance, observe the massive outbreak of rape and of other violence being done to women by men, and also the increase of vicious crimes being done to men by the women, and then let us ask ourselves the question: *Whence cometh such hatred being done by man and woman to each other?* The voracious increase of these crimes, especially the crimes of rape and of child molestation, of brutish assaults between man and woman, are the direct result of the Human reproductive urge having been thwarted and cast aside thru the process of abortion.

When a normal biological urge is artificially suppressed then it will find expression in a warped or perverted manner, so that the mere knowledge of reckless and wanton abortion is itself enough to weaken and twist wrongly all the Human bonds between man and woman. The mere knowledge of abortion, we must understand, the mere knowledge that abortion has been morally and legally approved is, by itself, enough to introduce a basic rottenness into all else of Human integrity. This is, in fact, precisely what is happening around us at this moment.

Once we attack our own most central core of biological existence, and when the centre cannot hold because of that attack, then all other things must likewise fall apart. Once the practice of abortion has been morally and legally approved, then all other sins and further grief must necessarily begin to increase, to multiply upon themselves.

Where, O where has love gone nowadays, boys and girls? True love has been flushed down the toilet, along with those millions of dead babies we have aborted. This has been done in furtherance of what we have imagined to be freedom and liberation. Instead, we have received massive death and the stench of dead meat from within the most secret garden of the Human soul. Thus the love of abortion has stolen away all honest pleasure from the bed of Human desire.

And I am not speaking here of abortions that are done because there has been a rape performed or when the pregnancy has come as the result of incest, or when it is known that the unborn child is hopelessly diseased or malformed, or when there is a clear danger to the life of the mother. Rather, I am speaking of the abortions which have come from adultery and from irresponsible sexplay, or because of political policies or esoteric philosophies about free choice that have nothing to do with the natural laws of Human biology. Life exists so as to recreate itself, and when that recreation is denied then that life urge will begin to die, and that death of the life urge is exactly what is happening at this moment both within and around all of Human society.

Do unto others as you would have done unto yourself, for that is what occurs naturally as the natural result of cause and effect, of action and reaction being constantly expressed and fulfilled. Therefore if abortion is what we give to ourselves, then it must necessarily follow that an equal abortion is what we shall receive as individuals and as the species entire. Death is death and abortion is abortion; whereas when life is enthused then further life shall come. Are we so ignorant, *Homo sapiens*, as to feel free to obviate and to otherwise interfere with the basic reproduction of our own kind, and that this interference is, somehow, good? Are we that ignorant, to believe that such is the case? Are we really and truly that ignorant, that stupid? Or, is this more of a fear reaction to the question of our unresolved doubts concerning the future of Humankind, and so is done at a time when the true path of species growth is not yet fully realized?

Here we are, a species of beings who are just a little bit bigger than ants on the ground. And so now we pretend to believe that we can spit with contempt into the face of our Creator and that we can bite the very hand that has fed Humankind thru out the millennia of Human existence, and that we can violate the very essence of Human biology by aborting our own babies, for whatever reasons.

Did we truly believe that there would be no consequences or ill effects resulting from such arrogant thought and foolish actions? Do we honestly believe that Human society could legalize and morally justify the massive aborting of Human babies yet still maintain Human sanity and personal integrity, while having the joyful pleasures of living left undamaged? Do we really believe that we can do such an ugly deed and that no one, not even ourselves, will even care or be adversely affected thereby? Human abortion, which represents the death of Human biology and of Human hope, must produce some deadening effect on the souls of the aborters, after all. That deadening effect must and shall be equally abortive to the souls of those involved, because the law of cause and effect says so.

Who is doing these abortions? Let us look in a mirror, *Homo sapiens.* Let us look at the faces of those people whom we see everyday, and what do we see? Beautiful women and handsome men tho we might seem to be on the outside, and yet how empty inside, how devoid of any zest for living and for the true lust of life to be lived we actually have become, because of this love for abortion. What sterile and impotent creatures we have become unto ourselves! We cannot reproduce our own young, or have refused to do so, with this love of abortion in mind. How dead to true passion we seem to be today, how absurd have the purposes of life become unto us, how wasted away are the lives of Humankind, and all coming from our love of Human abortion.

The knowledge of that wastage, the knowledge of these aborted Human babies and of the loss of all hope that has been thereby engendered, resides within us. That knowledge reveals itself upon our faces, in unguarded moments, as the look of blank despair. I see upon the Human face nowadays an awareness of death approaching, of an utterly dead stagnation newly laid down upon the Human soul. This comes from a fear of failure among individual persons and from the fear of an unknown future for all Humankind as well. This comes both from the general fear of darkness and from a basic and primordial fear that we cannot be successful against that darkness which lies beyond Luna.

Ergo, this generation of <u>Homo sapiens</u> *is behaving as moral cowards do: We are shrinking inwards and backwards from our natural destiny as an evolving species; we are polluting our own home planet; and we are aborting our own babies and we are continuing the preparations for nuclear war between the nations of the species entire simply because we are afraid of, and do not yet understand, the nature of our own ongoing growth.*

Yet even so, the will of Creation ordains that we shall not abort our unborn babies for no good reason, as we ourselves are but the children of Creation and of Mother Earth. We shall not slay the future growth, the life and the hope of any Human life yet to be born from *Homo sapiens*.

We shall not die now. As an alive and growing species within this galaxy of stars and planets, we shall not die now, but we shall go forth from this cradle of Earth. We must grow because our growth in nature is not yet fulfilled. We shall not die now, we shall not abort ourselves in fear and terror of the dark, but we shall go forth into the darkness and we shall give light unto that darkness, and our light shall be greater than that darkness until the darkness is no more.

We shall not die now. We shall not die now! We shall not die now but we shall go forth, we shall go forth and do our work. We shall struggle and we shall take our pleasures as we may. We shall fight. We shall think and we shall learn and we shall teach. We shall do farming and gardening. We shall build civilization and we shall seek Truth. And we shall make fire. When death comes we shall go forth even after that day to seek more life and greater light, but we shall not abort ourselves nor be aborted, but we shall go forth and be free among the stars until we have grown beyond them and burn with greater fire.

Chapter III:

The World Union

A Parable About Ducks

I once saw a Walt Disney animated cartoon wherein the plot revolves around the ongoing efforts of Donald Duck to further his courtship of the very beautiful Miss Daisy Duck. Apparently, Donald has asked Daisy to come to his house tonight for a romantic, candlelit dinner and she has accepted the invitation, so that the anticipated joy of pure love is swelling large in both their duckish hearts. The action of this cartoon playlet has to do with the efforts of Donald to make his house clean and tidy, and to begin preparations for the intended repast.

But Donald Duck is the eternal clown, and so his efforts seem always to go astray. When he starts to straighten up the closet, for instance, all the contents of the closet spill out until he is covered by the falling debris. As he tries to make up the bed he soon finds himself entangled head to toe in the sheets and blankets. When he steps on one end of the broom the other end pops up to knock him on the side of his head, and when the wind causes an open door to swing shut then the swinging door, of course, must slam into his backside. It is this type of constant buffoonery that provides the slapstick humor of the piece.

Very early in this story an element of suspense is introduced into the comic sequence. As part of his preparations for dinner, Donald puts a can of chili beans on the stove and turns up the heat. So great is his haste, however, so much of a clown is he, that he somehow forgets to pop open this can of beans. These beans, stewing in their spicy tomato sauce, are being cooked in a closed container where there is no way for the mounting pressures caused by the rising heat, and the resulting expansion of the stuff being cooked inside, to be safely released and vented away.

While Donald continues his housecleaning we see frequent glimpses of this doomed can of chili beans, as the can begins to show visible signs that internal pressures are mounting to an explosive climax. Finally there is a knock on the door, and the beautiful Miss Duck has arrived. Somehow, and in spite of Donald's clumsy efforts, the house has been cleaned and made ready for this romantic rendezvous. At the very moment when Donald throws open the door, however, and as Daisy steps into the room, with all the intentions of true love soon to be fulfilled showing plainly on both their happy faces, this famous can of beans explodes.

What a mess has now been made! The food is gone, splattered all over the walls of the kitchen and living quarters. The romance of the evening is likewise gone, and the mood has now changed into feelings of embarrassment and irritated chagrin. The farce of the comedy has been revealed, and there is nothing left but to end this charade and hope that happier days might yet come to be. All the good beginnings have turned into a bad ending, and simply because Donald Duck forgot a basic law of thermodynamics: That when heat is introduced into the closed system of a sealed container, then the pressure caused by the expanding gasses will begin to mount within the container and must be safely released, or else a catastrophic restoration of balance between internal and external pressures must take place.

This planet Earth— a closed system which contains the rising pressures caused by the expansion of one hot question after another and with even hotter questions still cooking on the back burners of the same old stove, and all these questions demand some urgent resolution, but no resolution has yet been found and no one knows what to do next or where to go from here, yet some answer must be found or else catastrophe must soon come instead, and each of us knows or senses deep within the very marrow of his or her bones that this is true— reminds me very much of that closed can of cooking chili beans. We are living in this same type of sealed container, and some means of easy venting for these expanding pressures must be opened and exploited fully or else an explosive release of those pressures will be forced upon us, to our dismay and loss of all good fortune.

But we have landed on Luna now, we have taken our first steps upon a planetary body other than Earth, and surely there must be an indication here as to the direction for any further growth of *Homo sapiens*. Because of those first steps, and the efforts required to take them, we are not the same race of beings today as we were 100 years ago. The blue sky above us is no longer the limit of Human aspiration. It must be apparent to one and all that a wider range of life has been ordained for the Human child. Fundamental questions concerning the Human condition, questions which have been asked since before the first pyramid was built or the Great Wall begun must now be answered, so that Humankind might grow and mature with the coming of the ages.

As we now stand face to face with the darkness that surrounds this planet we are also confronted by a veritable whirligig of problems to be solved, a multitude of difficulties so varied and so intricate, a stampede of wild horses who seem to be beyond all reason and hope of restraint, that I know at least one blind man who has a rough time in trying to shake a white cane at them all, or even to attempt the comprehension and full grasping of them. It might be of some assistance to us, therefore, that we corral and enclose these various problems into a limited number of broad categories so as to give a solid shape and substance to all our vague fears and high hopes, and so to reduce their many variations into a more manageable number. When we are faced with a multitude of confusions then we must, so as to understand and answer them all, try to reduce this infinitude of questions down to a finite number of most essential problems. Solve those problems first and then go forward from there.

First and foremost, our homeworld must be cleaned from the effects of industrial pollution. The rivers, lakes and the deep, dark blue ocean of Earth shall be purified from the various poisons which we have introduced into these waters of the planet. The forest woodlands shall be maintained by us and made healthy again. The fresh air that we breathe shall be made fresh again, freed from the stench of oily filth. The agricultural farmlands shall be made to yield a more fruitful harvest for the farmer. We shall rebuild our cities to make a better life for ourselves. This massive, global labor requires that our Technology be made cleaner, stronger and more fully within Human control than has so far been the case. The beginning of this labor shall be the further progress of our entry into this first millennium of the Human adolescence.

Second, we can understand how there must be some solid, consistent system to Human morality. There needs to be some general code of behavior among Human beings which is accepted as a standard by which to judge the good or bad manners of everyone, and is hateful to none. How can we understand life unless we first understand this much, at least: That individual Human beings must recognize each other as members of a sapient species which is united, historically and biologically; that we are now ready for more thought, action and further movement together; and that no further maturation of *Homo sapiens* is even remotely possible unless the individual beings of the species entire can learn, and agree to agree with each other?

If we cannot love our Human selves, if we cannot have some basic friendship towards each other, then how can we ever hope to love anything or any other living creature whatsoever? And if we cannot do that, then how can we live and be free? If we cannot even love the members of our own kind, then who shall love us?

Third, as *Homo sapiens* has now entered into an arena of darkness which has not only been unknown but also unknowable by Humankind prior to this day, and as the questions which now confront us are global in nature and in their full effects upon *Homo sapiens* as the species entire, then it must be clear to everyone that competing nation-states will no longer serve the needs of the moment. Therefore a World Union of political purpose and will, enthused fully by the desire that we shall govern ourselves as a free and living species of sapient beings, must now be in order.

A Response to Mr. Buckley: Christian Revelation and Empirical Observation

In the summer of 1996 I sent an information packet to William F. Buckley, Jr., in which I included a typed copy of the Preface section to *The Coming of the Ages,* as well as a computer disc containing the text of the first two chapters. My purpose was to try to arouse the interest of Mr. Buckley's conservatism, in hopes that he might pass the manuscript on to some literary agent, as if from one friend to another and that I might in this way find a secret passage thru the bureaucratic red tape of publishing an unknown author's first book.

In the covering letter of explanation I described the basic purpose of the first two chapters of this book and gave a thumbnail sketch of the intended third chapter, which at that time had not been written. As Mr. Buckley has long been a leading articulator of American conservatism and its relationship to 20th century geo-political history, I was hoping to pique his interest in these ideas and to secure his aid in furthering the publication.

On August 22nd, 1996, Mr. Buckley replied thusly:

> I've never had any success at all as a literary agent, but I should think there might be a market for your book. Father Teilhard is still awfully popular.
>
> However! You are very evidently very intelligent; I hope you won't mind a little cold water. Even supposing arguendo that most people on the globe agree with me about the value of the individual and his liberty, a majority of them are in thrall to those who certainly do not. The

warlords of China, for example, are unlikely to bind themselves to obey a global Parliament unless their vote is weighted by their population. I would decline to obey one in which it was.

Neither walking on the moon nor colonizing other systems alters teleology or the moral law. Feminism has been a long time coming—c.f. Mary Wallstonecraft; radical feminism may be a long time going, but go it will because it makes people miserable—c.f. George Gilder.

The idea that Humans are substantively evolving is contrary to Christian revelation, and to empirical observation. One of the most intelligent and enjoyable refutations of it is Chesterton's <u>The Everlasting Man</u>. Even if it did send you back to the drawing board, I think you would like it.

Yours Cordially,

William F. Buckley, Jr.

My goodness, but there are so many different hints and further indications contained in this brief letter from Mr. Buckley that I do not know quite how to respond to them all in proper order. This section of the book is mainly concerned with the political governing of Earth by *Homo sapiens* as the species entire. The time has come for Humankind to grow beyond the present rule of Earth by nation-states, and to establish the government of this first planet to come under full Human dominion. Before we proceed further in that direction, however, let us look first at these other comments and suggestions offered in Mr. Buckley's missive.

First, out of all the similar information packages sent that summer to various people and publications, Mr. Buckley's response is the only one to indicate that he had actually read the enclosed material. For that touch of Human effort I am very grateful to him for his personal integrity, and for his good intentions also.

"Father Teilhard is still awfully popular." I am happy to learn that the influence of Pierre Teilhard of Chardin still carries some weight in Human thought. His misfortune, apparently, was that he was born somewhat ahead of his own times, and it might be well for those of us who live in these days to catch up with him. His basic idea, that while we are the children of a divine Genesis we are at the same time the living beings of an animal species, and are therefore subject to all the normal laws of animal biology and survival, requires that our notion of God must be expanded so as to conform with this more exact view of true Creation. This perception must be of some aid and comfort to us in our efforts to understand just who and what we are, as well as to help us see the larger purposes of Human growth.

"Feminism has been a long time coming . . . radical feminism may be a long time going, but go it will because it makes people miserable." Yes, it cannot be denied that feminist ideals have been present for quite some time now. But we must realize that a full growth and climax of these ideas are not simply going to fade away and be forgotten for the same reason that a bell, once rung, cannot then be unrung. We understand that the Human journey to Luna and back signals the beginning steps of our growth into the age of *Homo sapiens* adolescence. We also know that the Human female tends to feel the onset of puberty sooner than does the Human male. When we further understand that what has been called Women's Liberation is but the sound of a biological clock ringing its bell for a wake-up call into a fresh day dawning, then we may also know that large and very basic questions concerning Human biology as well as Human history are at stake here, and not mere intellectual prattlings.

The Women's Liberation movement will not go away and be forgotten because this is a biological matter of species maturation, and will remain a part of the Human condition for so as long as man and woman endure and prevail together and mate with each other, even until we have been married into one being as *Homo sapiens* adult.

"The idea that Humans are substantively evolving is contrary to Christian revelation, and to empirical observation." Theological revelation is not meant to be an impossible barrier against the progression of Human thought. On the contrary, when we notice the constant forward motion of Human history, then we must presume that some far distant goal of mature growth is being approached. As Human knowledge is being slowly increased along with the increasing weight of Human experience so that more plus more of truth gradually becomes revealed to us, then from deep within the Human soul there must come a definite sense that the greater, deeper, wider and higher shall the fullest revelation be made known when our elder days come round at last, in full circle.

If we were to use whatever limits there might be in our current religious beliefs as a locked door which must not be opened, and with no regard for whatever further information might have been learned along the pathway towards that door, then where would we be now? We would be living on a planet that does not rotate upon its axis, is not in orbit around the sun, and the Earth would be a flat surface instead of ovoid in shape. Or else this Earth of ours would be resting on the back of a very large and slow moving turtle, and the vault of the blue skies would be held aloft on the shoulders of a Titan named Atlas, if Human thought were forbidden to pass any barriers set by previous limits of theological revelation, Christian or otherwise.

The quintessential fact, in Human history and in biological growth also, is this: *Homo sapiens* has now walked upon a planetary body other than Earth, while we could not have even begun to make such a trip during all the previous centuries of recorded Human history up until now. *We could not have even **BEGUN** to do so, I tell you!* Yet now *Homo sapiens* has done so, and in that one event there is all the difference between the ending of one age of Human history and the beginning of the next highest level of biological growth. This further development of the species entire is quite substantive, as real and as solid as a chunk of Moon rock which has been found and brought back to Earth from Luna, and was carried home in Human hands. How much more empirical does our evidence need to be, by the way, before we accept the solid truth of species evolution and education?

That we can now routinely fly beyond the atmosphere of our home-world and then return safely must be a sign that some growth has occurred in Human ability as well as in Human thought. How much empirical evidence must we see before we understand that *Homo sapiens* is an evolving species, and that the achievements of one generation are but the platform from which the next generation takes further steps? And more: That this continuation of growth is and must be the process of normal maturation of any living thing from childish innocence towards the more knowledgeable age of adult experience.

Suppose, by some unhappy chance, that Neil Armstrong's returning Apollo 11 spacecraft had crashed down into the very heart of Yale University at high noon. This would have disrupted that day's schedule of classes beyond all hope of any easy repair, I fear. Would the resultant brouhaha have then produced enough empirical evidence to persuade even the most jaded and blasé of observers that some crisis point in the long history of Human education and evolution had just now been achieved? I wonder.

If our expansion into this new Heaven and new Earth has occurred thru the biological evolution of *Homo sapiens*, or if these steps have been taken as the natural result of the constant education of our kind, then what is the real difference between those two expressions of animal growth? For that matter, who should even care? However we name the specific road by which we travel, is not the eventual goal of Human destiny still to be the same?

"The idea that Humans are substantively evolving is contrary to Christian revelation, and to empirical observation." Mr. Buckley, Mr. Buckley, Mr. Buckley! Can we not wake up and see the stars? O let us awaken and, forgetting for this brief moment these exact meanings of precise words, let us see these stars and know them as the horizon of a fresher, vaster sky than any we have ever known before, and then go forth regardless. Priests and scientists might argue these questions amongst themselves for many long years, and with some answers finally given, as it may be.

But the species entire should live and go forth from here, because there is no other answer at this time but that we must go forth from this planet and multiply, being fruitful. To remain as we are, overly crowded together on this small world and with a bursting population of Humankind constantly swelling, is to stagnate and wither on the vine for want of further room to grow.

For instance, we have heard accounts of ancient Rome, Greece and Egypt wherein those people traveled from place to place in their chariots, and that those chariots were pulled forward by teams of horses. Today those horses have been replaced by the internal combustion engine, and people travel towards and away from their homes in their automobiles. On the Apollo 15 mission to Luna the astronauts took with them what was called the Moon buggy, and in this new type of carriage they were able to travel in comfort across the lunar surface.

This Moon buggy, having been built to operate under conditions not to be found anywhere on Earth, was like but also unlike all the automobiles built during that same year in Detroit city, US of A. All of those cars in Detroit having been built to operate under conditions not to be found anywhere in the ancient world of 3,000 years ago, are like but also very unlike the horse chariots used in those days.

Each of these means of transport and carriage, from the chariot to the car to the Moon buggy, represents a progression forward from the limitations that were found in previous means of travel. This is how the other progressions of Human history are done: That as we live in one place and under certain conditions, we adjust ourselves to those various conditions so that then the natural education of Humankind naturally occurs, because the force of necessity propels invention, when those conditions are changed. These provoked changes, when they happen over long periods of time and are consistent with our own personal adaptation to the needs of an expanding Human life, make for the larger pattern of Human maturation. Does this have anything to do with the biological process of species evolution, or is this more a matter of normal species education?

There was a time when Human beings could not walk erect, had no organized system of spoken or written language and lived in caves, and could only live according to what protections and food they could find in their natural environs. Nowadays we walk upright on our two legs, which leaves our hands free to hold and use the tools that we make or can find by skill or good luck. With the learning of language we can communicate our thoughts quite freely amongst ourselves, and can pass our ideas and the memory of events along from one generation of Humankind unto the next. We can build houses and cities, and live in places that would not otherwise be hospitable to our kind. Does this represent the workings of evolution, or is this nothing more than basic education at work? Or are these two activities one and the same as each other, in that the constant education of *Homo sapiens* is a standard by which we measure the progress of species evolution?

As has been the case with the species entire, so also is the growth of a Human child towards adulthood. A newborn Human babe who cannot walk or talk, and is completely helpless to survive except in that the father and the mother will protect the child, is in the same condition as were our earliest and most dimly remembered ancestors: That we were completely helpless to survive except in that God and Mother Earth provided nourishment and protection to their newborn Human offspring, and allowed room for the infant species to grow.

This process of growth, from the infant *Homo sapiens* to modern Humankind, must be a sure and certain sign that essential growth of a species has taken place and that this growth has been caused by a continuing education and a cumulative increase of knowledge. Because of this cumulative increase in knowledge we find that we are now in a position to move from one whole environment into another, from Earth into the solar system and thence towards the galactic stars. Therefore Human evolution exists, and our current status in the slowly unwinding tale of Human history is clear proof of that biological fact of life.

"The idea that Humans are substantively evolving is contrary to Christian revelation, and to empirical observation." Mr. Buckley, we should be able to understand by now that to go beyond the limits set by contemporary religious theory is a process that continues forever, and derives from our own increasing awareness as to the Human condition. And this is but our own groping and stumbling towards whatever final, ultimate truth might one day be seen and known by the Human child. *Human evolution is but the constant process of species education, always going forward, and with the greatest of lessons saved for last.*

Let us remember the prehistoric generations of Humankind who flourished during unrecorded millennia upon the wide plains of Earth, dwelling in dark caves with no fire to warm them nor with any weapons to defend themselves save for native wit. Today we can see a vast Human civilization that has embraced the whole of this planet. Now we find ourselves reaching outwards to further embrace the moons and the planets of this solar system, and with increased hopes of moving outward towards the stars beyond these places. We know that our overpopulation of Earth has forced us, and with a primal force indeed, into this expansion of Human territory. Ergo, we must understand that the Human condition is substantively evolving, and that each of us now alive is a living agent of that process.

Responding Further to Mr. Buckley:
Concerning Dolphins and Eagles

"Even supposing arguendo that most people on the globe agree with me about the value of the individual and his liberty, a majority of them are in thrall to those who certainly do not. The warlords of China, for example, are unlikely to bind themselves to obey a global Parliament unless their vote is weighted by their population. I would decline to obey one in which it was."

This is very bad news indeed, and not only because of what these words say but also because of their source. It must be remembered that William F. Buckley, Jr. is not just an innocent bystander in these matters of global debate but is himself a man of letters and great learning, and that his advice represents a voice that is closely heard in all the national governments of the Western world.

How can Mr. Buckley, and by implication his philosophical compatriots as well, so casually demonize the political leadership of a vast nation such as China by simply dismissing them as mere warlords? Can there be no regard for the Human needs and aspirations which might be urging those people forward in their national goals, in much the same way that America's Human needs and aspirations urge them forward towards their own national goals as well? Is there no regard for the possibility that neither peoples is so thoroughly steeped in evil as each of us believes or pretends to believe about the other? Does he not realize that we all share in the same Human condition of life and death, in the same basic struggles for existence, and in the same wish to justify our existence with some good purpose achieved? If he and his cohorts do not understand these things, then this shows quite clearly that Humankind is once again involved in the ancient courtship ritual of war.

Nuclear war between the nations must soon come to pass and be upon us unless wiser counsels, political counsels which speak with advice that is based upon more mature, farsighted thought than has been heard up until now, begin to prevail upon the spiritus mundi and body politic of the species entire.

But *Homo sapiens* has now set foot upon Luna, has taken steps upon a planetary body other than Earth, and so the birth of a fresh perception of Human history is now in order. From the very moment when Neil Armstrong first walked upon the moon then the nations of Earth ceased to exist, except as to the geographical boundaries of various local populations. That we have now moved into a higher level of political awareness is a solid fact of life and of Human history, and cannot be simply ignored or passed off as just another routine event of life going on as before.

Looking back at Earth from the surface of Luna we can see no nations visible, but only a planet shining in the void. Here is the Earth of our beginning, the cradle of Human genesis. This planet, our homeworld, is to be governed by the will and the purpose of *Homo sapiens* in hope that Human truth shall not perish altogether but must flourish rather, and shall one day shed a great light upon the darkness of the void. With such thoughts as these in mind, therefore, the first World Union of Humankind is established, so that the will of the species entire shall be furthered by the collected desires of the gathered Human family, and thus shall the purposes of the body politic be known amongst us and made real.

During our earliest efforts of political order and social organization, single villages of Humankind were ruled according to local tribal law and by the will of the strongest family clans. Thence we continued onward thru the times when dynasties, monarchies and city-states governed Human society. Now we have again gone forward into the present day rule of Earth by nation-states. From this progression we can see that Humankind has always struggled, reaching outward to obtain larger and larger areas of political organization, so as to achieve a broader sense of central authority in the management of Human affairs.

As we now stand poised to take further steps beyond those first steps we took on the surface of Luna we must realize that, as a species, *Homo sapiens* stands alone in the midst of a vast darkness in which the very vastness of it all is utterly beyond our current understanding. Ergo, it must necessarily follow that we must stand together, and that this is not a question of mere morals only, but of the basic survival of *Homo sapiens* as a living species.

In all of this unknown, most vast and starry night of the universe which must extend beyond Luna, what can it really matter if these people or those people from Earth are Russians or Chinese in ancestry, or if other people are American or European, or if others are African, Israelis or Arabs, or if some others are Brazilian, or Japanese, or are Australians or Mexicans or Koreans, or are Eskimo and American Indians, or were born in India, or if there are religious and other cultural distinctions within our peoples?

We must know that these personal distinctions among ourselves, and these distinctions seem to be very large to each one of us as an individual being of *Homo sapiens,* are actually very small when compared to the far larger lives of the stars. All these minor distinctions derive from the same basic conditions of Human existence, and despite those distinctions *Homo sapiens* is, and must be, a gathered family of Human beings who are now involved in the greater maturation of our kind. Thus, as the biological entity of the species entire, we must now stand up as one peoples and rise together as a species in Union with itself.

Beyond this basic fact of historical truth, then, what minor and secondary questions are of any other significance but that the Human race shall survive on this planet and go forward from here? Of what great import are the microscopic differences between the individual molecules of an acorn, but that the acorn should one day sprout and grow into a thickened oak with many branches and leaves, then to produce and spread more acorns of its own? What does it matter if the caterpillar pupa in the cocoon should sleep and be ignorant of its own secret maturation process, just so long as the new butterfly then emerges to take wing and fly on high with quiet beauty? Who cares that the rosebud, tightly wrapped around itself and not yet understanding its own fullest growth should then unfold into its greater blooming anyway, if only that the beautiful, fragrant rose sends forth its perfume upon the summer winds?

Further likewise, what do our personal differences between ourselves matter whatsoever, but that we shall grow to send our Human radiations forth upon the solar winds when once our own adult growth is obtained and achieved? *Like these acorns and pupae and rosebuds, we are caught and are enthused with the process of our own evolving maturity. Like those other growing things we must continue as we have begun, even tho we do not yet understand the fullest possible achievement of that growth, but in hopes that the final goal of Human evolution must be of some good and worthy purpose both for ourselves and to fulfill the most basic will of true Creation.*

John Donne, the English writer, once observed that "No man is an island, entire of itself; every man is a piece of the continent, a part of the main; if a clod be washed away by the sea, Europe is the less, as well as if a promontory were, as well as if a manor of thy friends' or of thine own were; any man's death diminishes me, because I am involved in mankind; and therefore never send to know for whom the bell tolls; it tolls for thee." This is a clear and precise statement of an historical and biological truth: There is a large creature in residence here whose name is *Homo sapiens*, and each of us is a male or female molecule in the body of this greater being.

As when we reproduce the Human generations we remember our beginnings and see that there is and must be a continued growth, education and evolution of Human thought. There is a large creature in residence here, I tell you! And, as each of us stands and lives, then just so shall *Homo sapiens* live and be free to flourish.

Let us just take a look at ourselves, at our current condition and at the condition of our homeworld. Earth is congested, tightly packed with an overpopulation of Humankind, and the bruising friction of this constant elbow to elbow contact with each other has produced a global tension within the Human family that is utterly beyond all the previous experience of our race. The massive industrial polluting of our food, water and air supply, a contamination which has been ignored and left untreated by us up until now, has corrupted our planetary environment, our daily living and, I have no doubt whatsoever, has damaged our reproductive abilities and has warped our normal sexual desires into various perversions of natural function.

Also, as any reading of the daily newspapers as well as the events of public gossip must serve to inform us, we see that a full derangement of Human sanity is now in an active process of virulent brutality. We see that global madness has become a very real threat against the happy lives of all the many peoples of our kind, and that every member of *tutto populo* and *hoi polloi* has been affected badly by these toxic conditions.

The results of this process are most fearsome, odious to behold, and must cause the wisest of us to be quite suspicious of whatever apparent truths might seem to rule all current philosophies and everyday thinking. For in this poisonous atmosphere which we have made and wherein we live and breathe, what thoughts most poisoned might seem true to us and yet still be false, false and then most false again? Who can trust the judgment of even the judges, when the judges themselves are living within such poisoned environs as we have made for ourselves on this, our homeworld of Earth? And who will heal the sick, when even the doctors and nurses themselves are also dying?

Do you understand what I am saying here? Our food, water and air supplies have been corrupted fully! Under the theory that you are what you eat, it must be presumed that our finest ideals and the highest truths we are now defending have been similarly corrupted. The need to make a complete and fresh re-examination of Human history and of our own current motives has now been laid upon us by the first steps that Neil Armstrong took on the moon. In the name of all Humankind Neil Armstrong has stepped into a dark house so that we, *Homo sapiens* as a species entire, have not yet seen any light in that dark abode. And so we do not yet know where to go from here or what to do next, or why any further steps should be taken. To light this dark house that we have now entered, or at least to understand that such a light in the dark void is possible, is the fundamental duty of this generation of *Homo sapiens*.

Everywhere and in all ways, we feel the very real threat of a great war between mutually opposed nations, between political, religious or ethnic segments of the race, and even the potential victors of such a war must fear a victory wherein those who still live might well begin to envy the dead, and when so much of our homeworld must surely be burned away by nuclear fire. This planet is filled to the breaking point with the hatred and the fear of Human beings towards each other. No one feels safe or content or in hope of better days yet to come because *Homo sapiens*, as a gathered family of living beings, is afraid of Humankind. We Human beings are the very worst enemies of Humankind, for there is none for us to fear on this planet but ourselves.

Let us take another look at this passage from that letter, and then ask ourselves what these words might portend:

> Even supposing arguendo that most people on the globe agree with me about the value of the individual and his liberty, a majority of them are in thrall to those who certainly do not. The warlords of China, for example, are unlikely to bind themselves to obey a global Parliament unless their vote is weighted by their population. I would decline to obey one in which it was.

My goodness, Mr. Buckley! Do you believe in true democracy, or do you not? Do the various nations of Earth have the right to pursue their own national destinies, or do they not? What does this mean, then, but that the dominant political philosophy of American conservatism is nothing more than a new version of the me-good, you-bad type of thinking that motivates children at play in their games of cops and robbers? Do such thoughts as these truly indicate the fullest possible limits to, and the farthest horizons of, our vocabulary of Human political theory?

Or is it possible, and this sounds more close to the truth of everyday living, that the various political thinkers whose influence rules and shapes the political thought of the various national peoples of Earth today are but a bunch of moral cowards, and that their chief fear is simply that not all the various peoples on this planet speak the same language, or behave with the same social mores, or even that they do not wear their clothes in the same style of fashion as does everyone else? If this assessment is true, then merely because different peoples sometimes seem to be a little bit different in their living of life, a teeny-tiny, itsy-bitsy, eentsy-weentsy, wee little bitty-bit different in their various approaches towards true Creation, and that there might be but the width of a molecule between their various perceptions of Human integrity, then is it absolutely necessary that we of Humankind must now plot and plan to set loose the dogs of war upon ourselves and wreak a havoc of fire upon this small world? Or, that we are not, somehow, a collected peoples of the gathered family, *Homo sapiens* as the species entire?

Homo sapiens is of one flesh, one blood, and one soul! *Homo sapiens* is the species entire, and this species is made from the lives and the history of an uncounted multitude of individual beings. *Homo sapiens* was not born nor have we lived for so long as this, and according to the will of Creation, just so that we should now, beset by our fears of the universal dark and afraid to go further into that void in search of that brightest of lights that lives forever beyond that dark night, destroy ourselves on this small planet by global war and so give to ourselves a dead night on this Earth. *What is this nonsense, that we should rob ourselves of our own true birthright simply because we fear each other as different peoples of the same whole family of Humankind?*

Are there true causes for war here, or is this the mere lust of adrenalin passions at work among us? Grow up! The time has come for us, as a living species of sapient beings, to grow up, to wake up from our childish antics into the wider, deeper and more distant possibilities of our own adolescent growth and species expansion.

There must have been some progressive growth in Human knowledge, and in our search for the ideals of Human government, some gathering of an evolving education which has come into the mind of the Human body politic since those centuries and millennia when tribal warfare, raw and savage and transient on a daily basis, was the only means by which to establish any hope of social order. We must certainly hope that such growth has occurred, because this *ante bellum* path of global political policies herein advocated by Mr. Buckley is the same old path of tribal warfare, which we have already walked so many times before. Yet now we must see that these tribal wars being fought between opposing nations are, in fact, being fought within the one great gathered tribe of *Homo sapiens*. The next major war on this planet will be a nuclear war where *Homo sapiens* might wound itself to the point of species suicide. We might just as easily blast ourselves back into a Stone Age darkness, forced to hunt in packs and live in caves again.

The intelligentsia of Humankind in America, Russia, Europe, China and everywhere else on the planet, honest thinkers tho they might hope to be, have ignored the significance of this basic fact of recent Human history. *Homo sapiens* has now walked upon the surface of Luna, to enter into a wholly new territory of limitless horizons wherein everything is fresh and clean again. Wherein also, all past sins must be forgiven and forgotten in the exuberance of species expansion and star-filled serendipity.

As for the communists and the capitalists, who should even care about them? Who should care about them one way or the other when we now have the light of the stars themselves to pursue, the dark void to explore, and a cornucopia of fruitful new worlds to discover and colonize as we may? Who should even care about such local and mundane political conflicts that confront us nowadays, except that these conflicts be resolved soon and with firm resolution?

Who are these warlords of China, anyway? Who are the warlords of America, of Europe, of Russia, and of the rest of Humankind? Are they not like unto each other, seeking the same answers to the same basic problems that every nation or group of nations now faces, and are we not all members of the one gathered Family? By what magical process have other people become imbued with all evil intentions, while everyone else claims to represent all the virtues of moral goodness? There is a heavy overload of big weapons and their very elaborate, tricky delivery systems now present, very ready to be used by the nations of Humankind against each other on this small world. Yet this is the only planet now available to us, and able to support Human life. Thus we must realize that blaming each other for those sins of Human frailty which we all possess, while at the same time we pretend to be ignorant of the Human virtues in which we all share, is very stupid stuff indeed.

Since the beginnings of spoken language, how many teachers have there been who espoused the desires for harmony, understanding and the basic love of Human beings for each other? How many martyrs to this cause have there been? How many inspirational books and poems have been written, how many great works of art have been done, how many eloquent speeches have been made on this subject, and all to no avail? All to no avail, apparently, because the same old wars continue to come with monotonous regularity.

Observe the dolphin and the eagle, how different the one is from the other, how their natural environs preclude any true meeting of the minds between them. While the dolphin lives and swims within the ocean depths, and as the eagle flies high among the clouds, then of course there can be no union of thought or action between them. What might be right, true and of great import for the one would naturally be of no interest whatsoever for the other.

But such is not the case with *Homo sapiens,* for we are of one kind. We all eat food, drink water and breathe air; we are all subject to the same basic laws of gravity and motion; we are all born from the marriage of man and woman to each other; and we are the flesh and blood of *Homo sapiens.* We have been informed as to the source of true Creation, and we know that the fire of true Creation is brighter than the fire of the stars themselves, and that this fire dwells eternal within the Human soul.

Is there any real difference between our many styles of political government, our various systems and theories of economics, or between the great churches of our Human religious experience? Since these ideas have come from the same basic Human soul, and since these institutions have all been established so as to answer the same basic Human needs, then all these types of governmental policy, economic theory and religious practice must fall within the same broad range of Human reason and understanding. Since we all are Human beings, then how can any of us make or do anything that is utterly beyond, or outside of, or completely alien to the biological limits and horizons of the total sum of all Human experience? Can a dog, for instance, do anything whatsoever that is completely undoggish? Likewise are the communists and the capitalists really and truly that much different from each other, or are they both merely aspects of the same basic Human condition?

We are not dolphins and eagles, who cannot understand each others' needs and desires! We children of *Homo sapiens* are of the same kind. And now that we have traveled beyond the limits of our homeworld, now we must expand our Human awareness, so as to conform with the expansion of Human territory made real and solid by those first steps taken by the first Human being who walked on Luna.

All the arguments and the hatreds that have divided us are of our own making, and spring from our fears of ourselves and of each other rather than from the uses of mercy and good reason. These quarrels have been made in direct defiance against the teachings of Siddhartha Gautama, of Socrates, of Moses, of Jesus, of Mohammed, of Abraham Lincoln, of

Count Leo Tolstoi, of Mahatma Gandhi, of Martin Luther King, Jr., and of Father Pierre Teilhard de Chardin, to name but a few. I wonder if, in all the halls of Human government, we really and truly believe that we can continue to make these massive wars between ourselves and to use these weapons of utter devastation against each other, while we stand with such a complete disregard for all the basic laws and teachings that have come to us from the elder prophets of Humankind. Do we really believe that there will be no punishment invoked for such willful and blatant transgressions against the Human soul and against the will of most pure Creation also?

Do we truthfully believe that fiery war within the bowels of Human civilization is somehow the path towards salvation and the redemption of the Human soul? We hear talk of warlords, warlords, and more warlords all over the place! And I am sick unto death from all this talk of warlords! We are our own warlords, and we are making war upon ourselves and within the Human family, Mr. Buckley. It must be obvious to one and all that the time has come for *Homo sapiens* to make an active, conscious pursuit of a fundamental political union within the Human body politic.

When all impossible answers have been eliminated then whatever answer yet remains, however improbable that answer might seem to be at first glance, must be true. Ergo, the World Union of Earth, and this Earth of our beginning is but the first planet to come under Human dominion, shall be established, ordained, and inaugurated forthwith.

Further Responses to Mr. Buckley, with Digressions

"Even supposing arguendo that most people on the globe agree with me about the value of the individual and his liberty, a majority of them are in thrall to those who certainly do not. The warlords of China, for example, are unlikely to bind themselves to obey a global Parliament unless their vote is weighted by their population. I would decline to obey one in which it was."

I recall from my youth a time when my family lived in a neighborhood which was plagued by the antics of a noisy, bothersome dog. This dog took delight in chasing cars, pursuing and harassing every driver relentlessly. This was a cause for some concern and worry from everyone, including my father and mother, who were afraid that in attempting to avoid hitting the dog they might hit a child instead, or swerve and hit a parked car or a tree or whatever, and there came to be a definite sense of resentment within the neighborhood towards this dog.

Eventually, of course, what had to happen finally did occur. The dog got careless and overly enthusiastic once too often, and was struck with a good solid bump by a car he was pursuing too closely. The dog was not killed, but when he reappeared in public a week later he walked with a decided limp. He had grown wiser from the experience, however, and his harassment of passing cars was now limited to barking and growling, but from a safe distance away. Apparently, then, this dog had learned a valuable lesson in life: That when one is close to where massive weights are in constant motion and where heavy forces are in frequent use, then one must take care and remember caution.

It was amazing to me, and both my father and my mother commented upon the fact, how one incident of shock and pain could have altered the dog's behavior so thoroughly. The memory remains with me to this day as a flesh and blood example of one true aspect, at least, of an educational process at work.

Now let us look at the history of *Homo sapiens*, how we have injured ourselves by provoking one war after another, after another and then again after another. All these wars have been internal conflicts within the body of the gathered Family. We are even at this time moving in hot pursuit of whatever war is next to come. That war cometh soon unless some deeper thought of care and caution is taken by this generation of Humankind. Most of the miseries of the world have been caused by war, and when the war ends no one has ever been quite certain as to the cause of the war, and so the same conditions which led us to the last war continue to urge us towards the next affair of fire and ruin.

We have memory of these events! We are not living in a vacuum of knowledge wherein all past experience is unknown to us. We know what pain we have caused for ourselves in the past and so, as a species of living beings who are endowed with the potential for creative intelligence, it is both our duty and our honest desire that we learn from the painful war-bumps we have experienced in the past so that we might then be able to avoid that same pain in future days.

If a dog can learn such a lesson after only one brief encounter with a fast moving car then cannot the Human race, which has suffered at least a dozen such bumps in this century alone, learn the same lesson? This essential question is the basic intention of my story: Is the whole Human race, with its collected memory of both war and peace, as smart as a dog in the street?

We know what war does. We know what massive weapons of total annihilation we now possess, and we also know that there are some among us who are most eager to use those weapons in the adrenalin fury of immature passions. But if a dog can be slammed just once by a speeding car, losing all interest in chasing those cars ever again and thus learning a valuable lesson of life, then cannot we learn the same type of lesson for ourselves?

That is what I really wish to know, Mr. William F. Buckley, Jr.: Is *Homo sapiens* as the species entire, and we have just recently left our homeworld to walk upon Luna, and who must now engage in global labor so as to cleanse our planetary life-support systems from the effects of industrial pollution, and who must establish a global Parliament wherein the various political questions among Humankind might be resolved, smarter or stupider than a dog? This is the question we must answer for ourselves: Is *Homo sapiens*, as a gathered Family of sapient beings, smarter or stupider than a mongrel dog running wild?

I know now, Mr. Buckley, that the time has come for us to avoid the influence of these many and diverse warlords among us, to eschew their efforts all together. *Homo sapiens* must have learned something during the last few thousand years of Human experience; because, of what other value is Human life if not to learn, and then to profit from that knowledge? These various warlords, Chinese or otherwise, have pushed Humankind into one war after another. Can we learn from past experience, and can we build a global Parliament of Humankind, the World Union, a World government that shall have full control and discretion in the making of war? These local squabbles between nations must cease, so that *Homo sapiens* can be safe and secure on our homeworld. Only then, and as a united species, can we go forward hence to discover and explore the furthermost limits of Human civilization. But first we must solve our own local problems, simply because they are our own problems, *sonna cosa nostra*.

Towards what good purpose, for instance, did Mohandas Gandhi come to speak his teachings in India? There is disease and starvation everywhere in that land, and there are no modern toilets or any adequate system of plumbing nor any Human waste treatment facilities nearby. The rivers there, including the sacred Ganges, are among the filthiest waterways on this planet.

See how the government of India has expended its national wealth and natural resources so as to build an arsenal of nuclear bombs in eager anticipation of unleashing those nuclear fires upon their neighbors in Pakistan. On those days when he went forth to speak, Mahatma Gandhi could just as well have stayed at home in bed for all the good purposes of further Human education his words accomplished.

In Pakistan the people live in a squalor just as wretched as any to be found in India. The major cities of both nations are filthy beyond compare. The rats who live in the sewers there are healthier and better fed than are most of the people, and epidemic diseases are an everyday occurrence. Human life is neither happy nor healthy, but is instead a woeful burden and a bondage for living beings to bear. Instead of trying to move themselves forward into the new millennium by making any basic effort to cleanse themselves, their cities, their lands and their own homes, the Pakistanis have likewise squandered their own national treasury so as to amass a nuclear weapons arsenal with which they intend to exterminate their neighbors in India. How delightful! They have been inspired to do this, I have no doubt, by their religious contemplation of the Koran. If Mohammed were alive today, I wonder, would these deliberate plans for war between neighbors against each other be according to his desire or even to his liking?

Why does it seem so easy for us to find delight in the deliberate deaths and agonies of grief, and the devastation of Human civilization that must surely come to pass with the advent of a nuclear war between India and Pakistan? Why is it so difficult for us to live in harmony with our neighbors, especially when everyone involved, attackers and defenders alike, are members of the same whole Family? Are there no righteous people in those nations, people who are capable of righteous thought, living within either one of those two countries and able to make decisions, and who can foresee the bad consequences of wrong actions?

We must not be so wedded to the idea of war and massive bloodshed that we automatically run in that direction at the first sign of trouble.

Surely, there must be other ways to pass the time, ways and means by which we might expand our notions of true civilization. Turn your minds towards the building of underwater farms, so that you can reap a harvest of food from the ocean and thence feed the starving multitudes. Build more schools and hospitals. Clean and refurbish the cities. Clean the lakes and rivers. Learn how to remove the salt from ocean water, so that you can irrigate your vast deserts and make them into fertile farmlands, fruitful gardens of food and Human desire.

There is room for the growth of empire in these regions. There are more than enough people living there who would be willing and eager to do the necessary labors required for the building of empire when once the goal of such labors has been seen and understood. Instead of making wicked plans for aggression against each other, why not try to help ourselves instead? Why not make an active, deliberate effort to shun these weapons of war, and urge our neighbors to do likewise, so that we might move into the new age with a more mature sense of direction and purpose of will?

Mahatma Gandhi and Mohammed would both recoil in horror to see how the peoples in those nations have beggared themselves so as to gain the military might with which to obliterate each other's finest hopes with nuclear fire. Let us show mercy for ourselves instead. Let us use our various talents and wealth to build a better life for ourselves and for our children also. What is the good purpose of being Hindu, or Moslem or Buddhist, if our highest goals are but to murder each other by the thousands, and even the millions? We can find a higher sense of religious truth even in a pack of hungry wolves, and surely *Homo sapiens* can do better than that.

This is what I really wish to know, Mr. William F. Buckley, Jr.: Is <u>*Homo*</u> <u>*sapiens*</u> *as the species entire, and we have just recently left our homeworld to walk upon Luna, and who must now engage in global labor so as to cleanse our planetary life-support systems from the effects of industrial pollution, and who must establish a global Parliament wherein the various* *political questions among Humankind might be resolved, smarter or stupider than a dog? This is the question we must answer for ourselves: Is <u>Homo sapiens,</u> as a gathered Family of sapient beings, smarter or stupider than a mongrel dog running wild?*

Now we can also see thru out the nations of the Middle East where the Islamic peoples have been likewise blessed by the words of the Koran, that even vaster amounts of wealth have been spent in preparation for heavy war against their fellow Humans. In all that region there are likewise no modern toilets, no adequate system of plumbing or any Human waste treatment facilities, so that again the rivers have become choked with filth and the water is unfit to drink. Garbage is a polite term for the vile stuff that is dumped on the sidewalks and in the gutters of the cities every night. We see that poverty and disease are everywhere. The people live under conditions that are more squalid and wretched than are to be found among all the other creatures of the Earth. Yet even so, these people are enthused unto religious rapture by the thought of the slaughter of Israel.

We have even built vast storehouses which are filled with canisters of poisoned gasses and various chemicals of germ and virus warfare, so that we can slay fathers, mothers and their children as they lay sleeping in their beds, so vicious and mean-spirited have our religious fervors become.

These nations of the Middle East were given access to magnificent wealth by a lucky chance that huge deposits of oil are to be found within their national borders. Has this wealth been used wisely? Are the lives of the people made any better now, or are they just as wretched and miserable as they were before, if not worse? They have done nothing with their Arab money and their Arab gold! They have done nothing except to seek the deaths of their neighbors.

You have built castles and huge mosques. You have established lives of opulent greed and gluttony for the members of a few privileged families, but the vast majority of people in the Islamic nations continue to live in ignorance, fear and with an overall poverty of Human desire. Also we sense the loss of all hope that any better times might yet come to pass.

How is it that Allah is compassionate and merciful, but then we see that you have no compassion or mercy whatsoever, neither for yourselves nor for your neighbors? What mercy shall you expect to find when you have shown no mercy, but only fire and slaughter instead, to the living Human beings of your own species?

Why not use your wealth to try and improve your lot in life, to do good works for Humankind, to spread good cheer and fellowship within the family of the species entire, and to advance the cause of Human civilization? You can find ways to bring water to your desert farms, for instance, and irrigate those lands so that you might one day see vast gardens blooming where only barren sand is now. With your wealth, you can rebuild your cities so as to make them cleaner and healthier places in which to live.

You can do so many things and you can help yourselves in so many ways, but first answer this question: With all of the great wealth that has come from Arab oil, as you stand in the presence of those terrible weapons of war which you have built or which you wish to purchase with that wealth, as you contemplate the terror and the bloody gore that have been offered up as gifts to set before the shining throne of a merciful and compassionate Allah during the last 50 years or so, and as you must be aware of the fear and quiet desperation which you see stamped so clearly upon the faces of all those multitudes who now live in those military police states which you have forged for yourselves, then are you truly happy? In all the countryside and in the villages and in all the larger cities also, how many people in the Islamic World are truly happy to be alive, or are enthused with the simple pleasures of everyday living?

You have made Human life into a drudgery and a heavy burden to be bourn by this never ending cycle of brutal terror which you have inflicted upon yourselves, and upon the rest of the Human community also. The peoples of Islam need to read and then read again the Koran, and perhaps with a better understanding of truth, beauty, mercy, compassion, and simple Human decency to be learned than has been understood up until now.

Alas, O Islam, but what a shroud of dark shadow have you made for yourselves under the noonday sun! That shadow of gloom and foreboding shall remain, and the darkness in your heart of hearts shall not pass away, until you have learned to know that the individual males and females of Humankind are but the living members in the gathered family of *Homo sapiens*. When you give death to each other so freely, with no thought whatsoever as to the grief and desolation caused by these bombing attacks, by these rifle, pistol and sharp knife attacks, and by these poisoned gas attacks and the nuclear missile attacks also, then you are attacking and destroying yourselves as a living race of sapient beings.

"Praise be unto Allah, the merciful, the compassionate." If these words be true, if you believe in your soul that these words are true, then why not show some mercy and compassion for each other? Why not try to do good works for Humankind, and so help yourselves to find that light of true Creation which lies beyond that dark shadow of murder, grief, fear and ruin that now rests so heavily upon the mind of Islam? Why should so much of fear and horror have been thrust upon the global community by the readers of the Koran, a recital wherein so much of Human hope has been enthused? Those who have read the Koran need to read that book again, making a conscious effort to understand more about the current growth and changing of the Human condition.

To continue onward, let us look at the recent history of Korea

> Oh, East is East, and West is West,
> And never the twain shall meet,
> 'Till Earth and Sky stand presently
> at God's great Judgment Seat,

or so the poet wrote. But now that East and West of this Earth have met, and in Korea, the result was that a once united nation has been separated into two half-nations, and that those two halves have now been hostile against each other during the last few decades. But Korea will be reunited soon and be one nation again. It is towards that reunion of a single peoples with each other that we must now move, Mr. Buckley. These people are, after all else has been said and done, the fathers and mothers of each other. Naturally, they will not allow this separation of themselves from their own children to endure for very much longer. Ergo, some solid and most definite change of political policies must soon come and be pressed forward in that land.

There is always a risk involved when two friends are quarreling, and then a third party intervenes in support of either side against the other. The great danger is that when those two friends have reconciled their argument and have become friends again, they will then both turn and blame the interfering party for having caused the quarrel in the first place. This loudly shouted blame always comes regardless of what the original circumstances might actually have been true at the time. There is likewise the further chance that this third party, simply by remaining in the vicinity, will cause this disagreement to be prolonged far beyond the time when it would have normally been resolved had there been no interloper nearby.

This is the very situation that now confronts us as we contemplate the breaking of Korea into two separate nations of North and South, and as the presence of both China and America in that region continues to prevent or forestall any reunion between the sundered twain.

The Korean peoples make for a single political and spiritual union, both geographically and historically. We can sense that there is a yearning here, both in the North and the South of that nation, for a national reconciliation to occur. Also, the pressure for military action to be launched by either side against the other so as to bring about such a reunion by raw force, if necessary, continues to mount.

If America does not withdraw its military presence from the South, and if China does not cease from its political influence upon the North, then a war to restore Korean national sovereignty is inevitable. Furthermore, when the larger nations have been drawn into this local conflict, then who knows when or where the eruption of fire will end, or with what result?

Korea is not going to be forever divided into two half-nations. These people in northern and southern Korea are related to each other by blood and a shared history. It is certain that they will be one peoples again. This is a simple fact of current political history; so let us do ourselves a favor here, and take this fact into active consideration.

During this moment of Human history the time has come for the nations of Earth to unite themselves into a World Union, so that *Homo sapiens* might govern the World, simply because there is a biological unity that naturally exists between the members of a self-aware species of potentially sapient beings. Therefore all potential causes for war between the nations must be avoided, or else diverted into more productive channels of Human endeavor.

In both the northern and the southern parts of Korea, the political rulers have prepared for war. Each side, of course, has national allies who will help them fight this war. But ye must understand this, O ye children of Korea! When you allow your Korean homeland to be used as the chessboard whereon great nations play out their struggles for global supremacy, then your own Korean farms and other systems of agriculture, your own Korean fisheries, your own Korean rivers, lakes and forest acres, your own Korean churches, schools, hospitals and government buildings, and your own Korean national industries, as well as your Korean villages and big cities alike must be burned away during the ensuing conflagration, and that your own Korean chess pieces shall be among the very first to be taken off the board.

Are you really that eager, Korea, to be used as the pawns in another power struggle between America and China? Is that not exactly what happened 50 years ago? Was this experience so pleasant and delightful that you now wish it to happen again, except with more massive weapons of devastation to be in use this time around?

Please consider: *When big sharks are in a feeding frenzy, then very often the Pilot fish who had guided those sharks towards the intended prey in the first place are themselves caught up in the mad passions of sharkish hunger, and are also devoured. When this occurs, there is never any apology coming to the Pilot fish from the big sharks that ate them.* Are you all completely certain, you sons and daughters of Korean fathers and mothers, that you wish for your national history to move forward towards such an ending? I wonder, if the path towards a calm and peaceful reunion between North and South might not be a more righteous way to go, and be in your own best national interests as well?

The inevitable efforts of the Korean peoples to reunite themselves with each other must surely serve as a good excuse for an upcoming global war, a nuclear war at that, between America and China. This is the very kind of a good excuse for more war within the species entire that *Homo sapiens* needs to avoid at this time, or to divert away from ourselves, or to absorb within the Human mind as just another item of folly in the normal process of Human education.

Any fool or child can understand a threat when once the danger has gone past. The ways and means of wisdom, then, is to foresee and avoid a coming threat so as to be secure from any danger that might otherwise have come. *Ergo, China must cease to aid the people of northern Korea in their dreams of conquest, so as to avoid yet another pit of bloody Human gore. Similarly, American military forces must quit the southern regions of that land. Thus these peoples might be freer to re-establish their own national sovereignty.*

War is a very messy business. A nuclear war on the Asian continent or on the North American continent might very well ignite firestorms that are not so easily extinguished. With nuclear fires raging over two continents, with the nations of Europe being severely damaged during the same conflict also, and with the peoples of the Middle East being likewise involved in their own nuclear bombardments, then the very essence of Human civilization must endure heavy losses and suffer a massive wounding of the Human soul.

Does this mean that national policies must now be changed, and moved towards other directions? Of course it does mean just exactly that, and how could it be otherwise? *Homo sapiens* has recently walked upon Luna, and we thus now stand naked upon another celestial body than Earth. We are no longer peoples of nations but are instead the members of a biological species of Human beings who must learn to think in terms of whole worlds. To the best of our current knowledge we are alone in this dark void, so we must learn to live and stand together as the collected body of the species entire.

There must come a time in the natural growth of a sapient species when opposing nations or other groups of peoples, even as a means of mutual self-defense against each other, shall move towards a collected and gathered political union. Our history on this planet cannot much longer endure unless there be some central authority present.

There must and shall be a central political authority on this planet, a basic will and purpose of the Human mind to be put into full operation here, a stronger voice of united reason. This is but a smooth continuation and further flow of the Human history that has existed since the days when city-states and nations first began.

There is a larger progression of Human history that is being enacted here, and we of *Homo sapiens* who live today are but the smaller players in this greater drama. At first, local law and order was maintained by the strongest members of local family clans. Those family clans eventually bonded together so as to form the foundation for the various city-states and dynastic monarchies, and these governments then maintained law and order within Human affairs during long millennia of Human days.

Homo sapiens has now moved forward to where Human government is conducted according to the economic and political needs of national states. However, the military competition between these nation-states must surely serve as the means of our own mutual destruction unless a strong central authority is now established here.

The progression of Human education and evolution moves onward, from the days when family clans governed Human affairs, to the days when the city-state was the basic guarantor of social organization, and now onto these days when the needs of the various nation-states carry forth with the governing of Human history. Today the first World Union of Earth shall be established and maintained in full good order. This is being done as a necessary part of a biological process of species expansion, and thus do we seek the furthermost perfection of Human civilization.

The Arabs and The Jews, in Zion

What are we going to do in that part of the world which is called the Middle East, where the peoples of Islam and the nation of Israel are so enthused with hatred and fear of each other, and yet everyone there lives in full worship of the one God of all true Creation?

These people have therefore come to overload themselves with various weapons of massive war, armed and aimed in fullest anger towards each other. This is in despite of the fact that everyone in that region is born from the same ancestry of Human religion, and yet they have learned to believe they are not. They have made themselves into separate nations and different sects instead, yet everyone there is a member of the same family of Humankind. This is a fact of religious truth and of Human biology also, which shall always be a fact regardless of what extremist and fanatic voices might shout to the contrary. We must now find the answer to the question: How can these people ever desire to find peace and contentment within themselves? How can they go forward from this place and be fruitful? Can there be any hope of salvation for the Human soul to be found and enjoyed, unless they can now learn to recognize themselves and each other as one peoples?

I have read both the *Koran* and the *Torah*, and there are no basic differences between them whatsoever, neither in their rules of dietary law nor in the idea of full submission to the will of the almighty Lord of highest Light. God is God for both the Arab and the Jew, no matter what the extremists might scream, ranting and raving. There is no basic difference here, nor can there be any basic differences among a clear-thinking peoples who wish to embrace and be enthused with the moral integrity of

175

Homo sapiens as the species entire. Do we all wish to enjoy a unity of purpose so as to share in the glorious labors of species expansion?

God is God, and whether we speak the name of Allah or Yahweh or of Christ Jesus there are no differences here, except as to local preference and tribal tradition. If this be true, then where is the debate involved? Where is the debate involved, except as to local and national territories of one small portion of this one small world of Earth? Where are the arguments between you, then, but that you have made these arguments for yourselves and for your own further confusion of wild passions?

All the nations of that region, those of Islam and of Israel, shall unite themselves into a new nation, the nation of Zion. The coming of Zion has long been foretold unto thee. The capital city of Zion shall be seated near Jerusalem, and this shall be a new nation upon the face of Earth, and there shall be the peace of the world.

And do not think or say to yourselves that this cannot be done! Have there been racial, religious and cultural hatreds that have whipped these people into bursts of frenzy and fury against each other during the last few thousand years? Yes there have been, and now the time has come for those childish squabbles to pass away. You people, you Arabs and you Jews, have educated yourselves and have propagandized yourselves into this messy nonsense, and so now you can get busy and educate yourselves and your children into a dawn of increased knowledge.

You are all children of the same flesh and of the same blood. You have all lived on the same land since before the beginning of recorded time. The one Maker of all things has also made all of thee, each and every one of thee. So now, instead of continuing to teach yourselves and each other and your neighbors and your friends the same old tired excuses for war, just get busy and teach each other and your children some Truth, for the first time in a very long time. And that, my fellow children of Creation, is how the nation of Zion shall come. Make the conscious decision to alter your thinking, and then conditions which you now believe to be permanent shall be swept away and be replaced by a fresher, cleaner sense of your own Human existence.

In these hurly-burly days we see a cornucopia of many diplomats and politicians running about, speaking forwards and backwards while saying this or that, seeking to sign treaties and other political documents which promise friendship but which guarantee neither any true friendship nor promise any end of hostilities. When everyone proclaims honest intentions, but we know in our Human heart of hearts that they are lying both to themselves and to everyone else, that all of those peace treaties have no more meaning than do vagrant gusts of wind amid a riot of earthquake, hurricane and desert sandstorm, then we must know also that *Homo sapiens* is moving towards great troubles ahead.

When we think about great troubles ahead and the coming of nuclear war then let us also recall the children's nursery rhyme,

> Humpty Dumpty sat on a wall,
> Humpty Dumpty had a great fall;
> Then all the King's horses and all the King's men
> Could not put Humpty Dumpty together again.

When we consider the destroyed cities, ruined economies, and the thousands upon thousands upon thousands of burned corpses that must result from any major war soon to be fought in that region of the world, then the story of Humpty Dumpty begins to sound less like a childish sing-along doggerel and more like an ancestral voice prophesying doom, does it not?

Mutually opposed nations can never have peace with each other unless there be some basic spiritual union between them, a joining together of the blood relations within the gathered Family, so that they see themselves as being of one peoples. So let Zion come! Let these nations of the Middle East unite themselves into a single Republic of Zion, where all disputed territories are blended and merged together so that all the land belongs to all the people, and there shall be a new nation upon the face of the Earth.

Homo sapiens is face to face with large problems in these days, problems concerning the biological health of our homeworld and of our political unity as a collected species also. At the same time we have launched ourselves into a virgin territory of species expansion that must proceed beyond those first steps we have already walked upon Luna. With such farther horizons of vision now laid open to our gaze, do we not begin to grow weary of such local disputes as we have recently seen between the Arab and the Jew? How can we find an end to these religious squabbles, ceaseless and unending as they seem to be?

What other end to those disputes shall there be but this: That these small nations shall unite themselves into the larger nation of Zion, a united Zion Republic with both Arab and Jew to be finally reunited with each other, rejoined and fully intermingled as they were 5,000 years ago? Now they shall be the same peoples again, including all of themselves into the common Union, thus to carry forward the collected will and further purpose of Humankind. What other answer is possible, but that there must be a political and a moral union between these enemy peoples, that they should come to love one another and to be one with each others' desire? With the same strength of passion that has pushed you all, Arab and Jew alike, into the bloody slaughters of each other during the last 4,000 years, then let the reverse strength of that self-same passion now bind you unto each other more closely, like Human magnetism attracting Human beings towards themselves and to each other.

The new Zion shall be bound together as closely as the peoples have been broken apart during recent centuries of war. There can be no forward movement in Human affairs until these barriers against the progression of Human thought that we, ourselves, have built and maintained are themselves now broken down, shattered and cast aside. It is the sons and daughters of this Human generation who must be the breakers down and casters aside, the movers forward into the wider range of life that has been ordained for thee. All past arguments between the Arab and the Jew will no longer avail; instead of thinking so hard about murder, ruin, wicked intentions and secret plots, mean actions to be done by each of us towards each other, let us do something good for a change, and let Zion come.

No other answer is possible; and once you have eliminated all impossible choices then whatever else remains, no matter how improbable, must be the truth. With that thought firmly held in mind, and all other possible choices having been eliminated by the exercise of common horse sense and a basic knowledge of Human history, then the political and philosophical union of the nations of the Middle East, where everyone speaks the same basic languages, and where they all worship unto the same idea of God, must be true.

Now, I am no expert authority in the political history of the ancient conflicts between the Arab and the Jew. All other political experts along with the various diplomats of the world have failed in their task to bring peace and concordance into that region. All their failings remind me very much of those same failed efforts of European diplomacy which led to the outbreak of the great war in Europe, in 1914.

Those fully trained experts of European diplomacy proposed and signed their many political treaties and made their many happy agreements between this or that nation, and these acts were done to the uttermost degree of wasted effort because the Great War came anyway. We can clearly see that the same march to folly prevails today, and likewise marches forward to the same bloody conclusions. We know that even more bitter dregs are to be found at the bottom of the same old cup of wine, and we also know that some amazing breakthrough must be made in these proceedings if Human history is to continue past this dangerous curve in the road.

Soon after that Great War had come to a dismal end, and with all the survivors feeling more befuddled and frustrated rather than either victorious or defeated, an odd conversation took place between two European diplomats. The British ambassador asked a question, "How did this sorry affair ever get started in the first place?" The German diplomat answered "Ach, if we only knew!" Imagine that, will you?

Just imagine that! A huge war had just been fought; millions of soldiers and civilians had been killed, with less thought than if we Human beings had been no more than mere cockroaches stepped upon by careless children at play. Whole cities were burned to the ground, entire national populations were laid waste by the epidemic diseases and starvation that swept thru Europe long after the actual combat had ceased, and there was darkness everywhere upon the land. There was also the smoke and stench of an Earth scorched by burning fire; there was the knowledge of ruin and the desolation of hope also, and no one ever knew why.

And to this very day, many years later, there is still no clear understanding as to why or how this great bloodletting in Europe and in Asia first commenced. "Ach, if we only knew!" If we could only know why we never knew, if we could only learn how to know better next time around, then the gain of that knowledge would be good, well worth the effort and all the blood that was spilled onto the ground, and worth all the pain, misery and grief endured, and the torture of the Human soul that was done during that war also, if only so that wiser and more mature thought might make an entry into the forehead of Human awareness.

This is the terrible thought that must concern us: Not that the war happened but that no one, even with the vision of hindsight to aid us, has ever understood the causes of World War I except as a series of gross political blunders, missed judgments upon each other's national intentions, and a tangled web of lies and malice which would make the tricky web of the most cunning spider seem simple. O what a tangled web we weave, when first we practice to deceive!

We stumbled into that war, just as ignorant children might bump into a hornet's nest or unwary travelers might fall into a pool of quicksand, and this stumbling and bumbling was done by those who were thought to be the shrewdest political thinkers of their day.

This thought must now trouble our minds, must give us pause in our thinking, and must give us further pause in our adrenalin passions for fire and the conflict of war: That if such an ignorant war could have been fought only yesterday, seemingly, and if that war was so stupid in its beginnings that no one has yet discovered exactly how it first began nor for what reason, then why should the same type of blundering war not happen again? When everyone is again enthused by the same mad desire to slay everyone else, and when everyone is again filled with the same type of rash angers but without knowing exactly why or towards what purposes, then that anger might soon come to erupt upon us like hot lava spewed from a live volcano upon the sleeping city below. How can this generation of Humankind make even the slightest pretense towards intelligent foresight when on at least one very recent occasion, in 1914, we led ourselves so badly astray?

I mean to ask this one question of *Homo sapiens*: *If Humankind made such a basic error in political judgment as occurred during the years and months and days leading to that Great War in 1914, and if no conscious increase of moral knowledge concerning right and wrong has occurred since then nor has there been any conscious increase of Human reason either, then why should we not be very much afraid that we are behaving, thinking and speaking just as stupidly, blindly and filled with the fire of hot wrath now as we were then?* We have been a species of unrepentant children, *Homo sapiens*, and we have been told by the prophets and elder teachers of the race that we shall make the peace within the family of Humankind. We still persist in making war over the various territories that in truth belong to all of us as the living children of Creation most pure. For *Homo sapiens* is the species entire, and the homeworld of Earth is our common dominion, so this planet must be saved from the devastation coming from our wars against each other. Upon this cradle homeworld of Earth most especially shall there be peaceful living, and we shall be the living beings of the species entire seeking the truth of highest Light.

But alas, how sharper than a serpent's tooth it is, to have a thankless child! What a generation of ungrateful whelps have we become today! We argue among ourselves and slay each other over the gifts that have been given unto Humankind from the one source of all true Creation.

Do they argue over ancient lands? Those lands do not belong to you anymore than do the waters of the river and the ocean belong to the fishes that swim thru them, nor does the air overhead belong to the birds who fly. All of life and of living is but a gift and a loan merely.

All that land of Palestine belongs to God. God caused the making of this planet; God has given that land unto these people and has allowed them to live there. What God has given God can take away again, and in the blink of an eye. These gross murders of farmers and merchants, of husbands, wives and children, and of soldiers using a multitude of weapons against each other and against the civilian populations of this or that nation, or of this or that church also, are but a blasphemy and a perversion of truth against the one true Giver of all gifts who is the primal Causer of all causes.

The very food that you eat is for free. You can grow your own food, you can go into the forests, the rivers, lakes and find food, or you can make your own food, or you can do work and earn money so as to buy your food in the marketplace, but food as well as the ability to obtain food is freely given from the great Maker of all.

The water that you drink is also there, and is free for all those who thirst for the cool liquid nourishment of H20, fresh and clean. The air that you breathe also comes to you without cost. Even gravity, and if there were no force of gravity at work then there would be no homeworld here nor any sun to shine with heat and light, operates only by the will of divine Creation. What more do you want, *Homo sapiens*? What more, thou ungrateful children whose offenses against true Creation are sharper than a serpent's tooth, dost thou desire?

With our landing upon Luna, *Homo sapiens* has been given access to the sun and the moon, as well as to all the various planets and moons of this solar system. Thence one day futurely we can seek, find and sometimes dwell upon the planets that revolve around the many stars that shine in the darkness of the void. What more, therefore, dost thou desire? Having been given so much, how much more elbow room do we require,

Homo sapiens, before we might try to calm our wrath against each other and then learn to live together as healthy children of the gathered family?

To fulfill the bounty of this most basic gift of life itself *Homo sapiens* has been asked, in words spoken by the prophets and teachers of ancient days, to think and behave yourselves in this way: That you shall love thy neighbor as thyself, and that you shall not do unto others what you would not wish to have done unto you. This is not a matter of mere piety and goody-goody babbling, or of the romantic idealism of dreamy poets, nor even of religious zealotry.

Rather, this is a basic law of biological survival: That either we shall learn to get along with one another as the living members of a free species, and inform ourselves into the biological body of the species entire, or Humankind shall be forced to walk a road that leads to the nowhere place of species extinction. Because, the same Lord of purest Light who gives life and the gifts of life so freely unto thee knows very well how to deliver total death also, and each and every living being of *Homo sapiens* knows that this is true.

We shall either seek and find the fullness of Human maturation, <u>Homo sapiens</u>, or we shall die as a species of sapient beings who have failed, who have shown themselves to be unfit for survival.

Homo sapiens! You will not be allowed to carry this heavy load of fear and hatred for yourselves and towards each other any further into the universe of Creation which awaits thee beyond those first steps which you have walked upon Luna, unless ye repent of civil war within the Family. God will stop you. God will stop you, and if you cannot come unto basic agreements with each other as living members of the same biological species, and as children of the same gathered Family, then you shall be withered on the vine just as badly ripened grapes are.

After all else has been said and done, then if we Human beings cannot learn to live with ourselves in some basic and primal union of biological accord, and if we cannot carry out our daily business and manage our affairs without murder, lying, theft, and adultery being done to ourselves by each other, if we hate members of our own species so much that we cannot live together with any biological union within our own animal kind, then for what good purpose is Human existence? Why should *Homo sapiens* be allowed to grow any further outward from this planet, if we cannot make this active effort to seek and to find a greater maturity of thought and action during this adolescent phase of growth towards the fuller blooming of the Human flower and fruit? If we cannot learn to forgive ourselves, then who shall forgive us? If we hate ourselves this much, then who shall love us? Where shall we find any redemption or the basic salvation from sin? Where shall be the glory of the Light?

See how the history of the Middle East has moved full circle, so that tho all things have changed during the last 5,000 years, yet all remains the same. All the original pieces have been returned to their original positions on the same old chessboard. Tho Pharaoh no longer sits upon the throne, the ancient peoples of Egypt are still here. The peoples of Iraq and Iran are alive and flourishing, as are those who dwell in Afghanistan, Jordan, Saudi Arabia and in Lebanon also. Those lands and those people have existed and endured since the very beginnings of recorded time. Even Israel, whose peoples were broken and scattered over the globe during the downfall of the Roman empire, has now been regathered as a nation and been returned into that region thru the natural flow of political history.

All of those various peoples who first lived in that same portion of the Earth 5,000 years ago are of the same blood. All of these people have come from the same small geographical location on this one small island of Earth. All are males and females of the same animal species. The religions of Islam and of Israel are so identical with each other at all their points of philosophical contact that they are as congruent as two dolphins who have equal length of years, size, weight and speed of swimming. How then could it be otherwise but that these various peoples are the spiritual and biological ancestors of each other, and that they shall now reunite themselves each to each?

Is there anyone here who cannot see that the hand and mind of true Creation has moved these people into a pattern of events, and that this pattern of events in motion is but the progression of a larger Cause whose full effect is not yet known by we transient mortals of the Human generations? Cannot we of *Homo sapiens* understand that it is the hand of God that stirs and flavors this same blend of Human soup? Are we so totally blind that we cannot see the operation of greater powers here, both within each one of us and all around us?

There must be some purpose that is being served here. There must be some reason and a divine Will that inspires Humankind into and toward this present climax of our biological evolution and greater education. In this present condition wherein such larger forces are in full play, do we truly believe that our own smaller passions and animal fears are of any significant import whatsoever?

Everything that you are or would ever hope to be comes from God, and all that has been asked of you is that Humankind shall make a deliberate and a conscious effort to be living beings of the species entire, and that you should not murder each other or steal from each other or lie to each other or commit adultery with each other's husbands and wives. The nations of this world, and the many people of Humankind, shall not make war upon each other but we shall make and recognize the global community of the Human race. This shall be the World Union. There shall be the peace of the world, the growth of the Human child up and into the deep, vast void which is beyond that first step we walked on the surface of Luna. Thence we may go forth and seek that eternal light which lies beyond all darkness.

Make Fire, and Goeth Thou Forth

Awake! for morning in the bowl of night
Has flung the stone that put the stars to flight.
And lo! The Hunter of the East has caught
The Sultans turret in a noose of light.
(Opening Quatrain to *The Rubiayat*, by Omar Khaiyam*)*

*So sorry, but this final section of **The Coming of the Ages** cannot be written at this time, but will be included in future editions. Meanwhile, the above quotation is just about the brightest good morning greeting I have ever read, and so you may enjoy that for now.*

0-595-19088-X